D0577550

TRUE CRIME

TRUE CRIME

Nick Yapp

This is a Parragon Publishing Book

First published in 2006

Parragon Publishing
Queen Street House
4 Queen Street
Bath BA1 1HE, UK

Copyright © Parragon Books Limited 2006
Illustrations copyright © Getty Images 2006

Created, designed, produced, and packaged by Publishing Projects Department, Getty Images

Text by Nick Yapp
Designer Tea Aganovic
Picture researcher Ali Khoja
Editor Mark Fletcher
Proofreader Liz Ihre

All rights reserved. No part of this publication may be reproduced, stored in a retrieval system,
or transmitted in any way or by any means, electronic, mechanical, photocopying, recording, or
otherwise, without the prior permission of the copyright holder.

ISBN 1-40548-540-X

Printed in China

Frontispiece:
The bars could belong to almost any "Death Row" in an American prison. The hands are those of Michael J. Bell,
awaiting execution in Colorado State Penitentiary in 1962.

Contents

Introduction

A police camera captures one of the most disturbing images of Charles Manson. It was taken by the LAPD in December 1969, just four months after the two-night killing spree by members of Manson's "Family".

The vast majority of criminals pass quickly through the justice system, receive their punishments and disappear into obscurity. A few become famous. Often this is because the crimes they have committed are so bestial or so heinous that the law-abiding world cannot forget them. That is how Ed Gein, and the Milwaukee Cannibal achieved their places in history. Others gain notoriety through their choice of victim. Few people today would know of John Wilkes Booth had he not gone to the theater one night and shot the President of the United States, indeed, many killers have chosen assassination as their particular crime simply as a means of achieving fame. Eighty years down the line, the name Bruno Hauptmann is still reviled because he was found guilty of the kidnapping and murder of an innocent child, the infant son of a great American hero.

And many criminals are remembered for other reasons. Rainey Bethea's unhappy claim to fame is that he was the last person to be publicly hanged in the United States. Leopold and Loeb, two smart boys, have been commemorated in film and song because their arrogance led them to believe that they could commit the "perfect crime", and then they betrayed themselves with a clumsy mistake that would shame the humblest novice crook. And many criminals – Charles Manson, Jack the Ripper, Al Capone – have gone down in history because for a couple of weeks, a few months, or a lifetime, their evil deeds held the world spellbound in fear and horror.

Men like these, and the few women that have matched them, rarely appeal for any attractive reasons, though some have passed into legend in the manner of Robin Hood or Till Eulenspiegel, snapping their fingers at society, living a devil-may-care existence, and luring the public into being momentarily on their side. Plenty of Americans were thrilled when Bonnie and Clyde or John Dillinger eluded lawmen, and some were even saddened when these desperadoes were gunned down in a hail of bullets. To the public, it was as though a great adventure story had come to a sudden end.

In general, however, the names of the killers and robbers, kidnappers and gangsters that have left a trail of corpses on the high road of history live on only in infamy. Here is a photographic record of what these people did, a rogues gallery of the culprits, and some brief attempts to suggest what prompted them to break the best known of the Ten Commandments.

Outlaws and Anarchists

Armed cattle rustlers cut wire fences on the Brighton
Ranch in Custer County, Nebraska, in 1885.

The myths and legends of the Wild West have been well served, and well plundered, by films, books, and songs. The same cannot be said for the truth. In a world where the Rule of Law had at best a precarious hold on society, the line between "lawman" and "desperado" was blurred. Men like Wyatt Earp, Wild Bill Hickock, and even Bat Masterson had days when they were gunslingers and law enforcers at one and the same time. Out of this confusion, it was popular opinion of the time that decided whether a robber, an outlaw, or a gunslinger was hero or villain, and back in the 1870s, 1880s, and 1890s, popular opinion decided that Jesse James was most definitely a hero.

James had the good luck to be championed by the press, in particular by John Newman Edwards, then editor of the *Kansas City Times*, and a man who campaigned for the return to power of old Confederate supporters in the state of Missouri. In a society of predominately small farmers, who loathed the banks that the James–Younger gang stole from, and had little sympathy for "Yankee" railroad companies and detective agencies, it took only rumors of good deeds on the part of outlaws to turn Jesse James and his like into Robin Hood figures, stealing from the rich to give to the poor. In the case of Jesse, the legend was completed by the manner of his death – shot in the back by Bob Ford, a treacherous member of his own gang, greedy for the reward offered for "Jesse James, Dead or Alive".

William H. Bonney, aka William Henry McCarty, but better known as Billy the Kid, was never so lucky. His was a sad and messy life, serving no popular cause, righting no wrongs, and doing little to help his fellow poor – not the stuff of which heroes are made. He was orphaned at the age of 13, and placed in a foster home by his stepfather. He fell in with a small time crook named Sombrero Jack, and first fell foul of the law by stealing laundry. He spent the next two

The Wild West

The "Dirty little coward, who shot Mr. Howard": Bob Ford displays the gun with which he shot Jesse James.

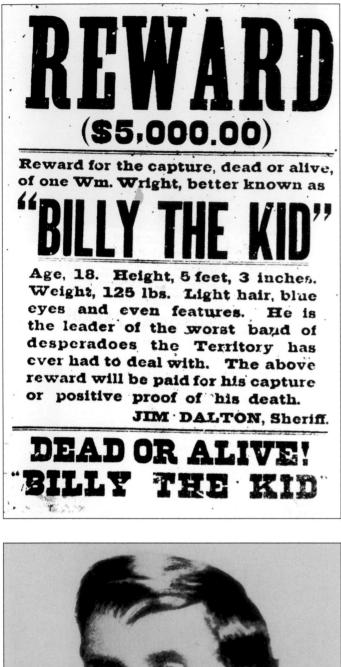

REWARD
($5,000.00)

Reward for the capture, dead or alive, of one Wm. Wright, better known as

"BILLY THE KID"

Age, 18. Height, 5 feet, 3 inches. Weight, 125 lbs. Light hair, blue eyes and even features. He is the leader of the worst band of desperadoes the Territory has ever had to deal with. The above reward will be paid for his capture or positive proof of his death.

JIM DALTON, Sheriff.

DEAD OR ALIVE!
"BILLY THE KID"

years tramping the country and working as a ranch hand and professional gambler, before teaming up with a horse thief named Jack Mackie. Most of Billy's companions were themselves pathetic creatures and unsuccessful criminals. Serious trouble came when he was 16. Billy shot and killed Frank "Windy" Cahill, a bully who picked on him once too often. Billy fled to New Mexico where he teamed up with Jesse Evans and his gang of rustlers known as "The Boys".

Unlike Jesse James, whose exploits were praised by the press, the teenage Billy the Kid and "The Boys" were denounced by Colonel Albert Fountain, editor of his local

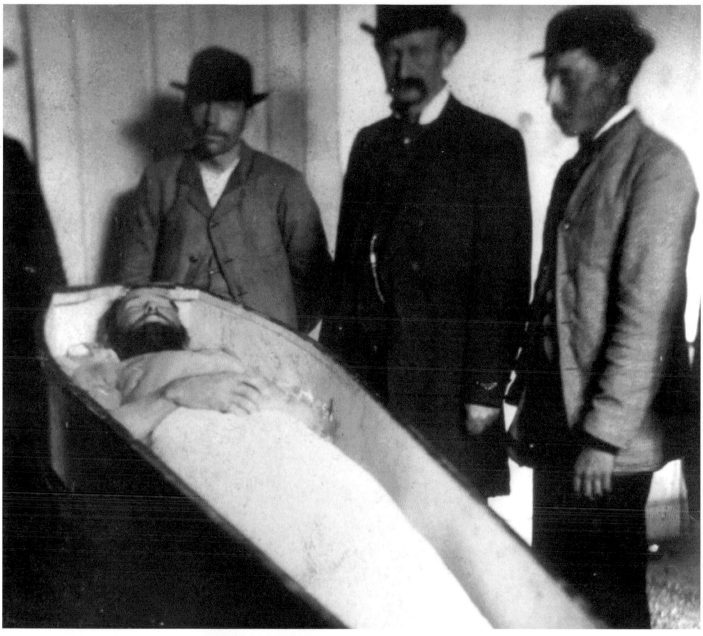

(*clockwise from top left*) A "WANTED" poster for Billy the Kid, issued c.1878. William "Billy the Kid" Bonney at the age of 21, with just a year of his life left. Frank James (standing center) stands over the coffin of his brother Jesse, Sidenfaden Funeral Parlor, St. Joseph, Missouri, April 4, 1882. A portrait of Frank James, dating from 1863. Jesse James, a year after his first killing in the raid on a bank in Gallatin, Missouri. Pat Garrett, the sheriff who tracked down and killed Billy the Kid.

REMAINS OF McLAURY-EARP
TOMBSTONE ARIZONA

Mesilla Valley Independent. Billy was repeatedly let down by life: deserted by his father and spurned by his stepfather; bullied by the first man he killed; betrayed by the Governor of New Mexico – Lew Wallace, author of *Ben Hur* – who had promised Billy exemption from prosecution following violence and murder in a power struggle between rival "rings" in Lincoln County; and finally killed by the man he had befriended and trusted, Sheriff Pat Garrett.

(*clockwise from top of page*) The Wild Bunch, c.1885: (*left to right*) Harry Langbaugh (The Sundance Kid), William Carver, Ben Kilpatrick, Harvey Logan, and Butch Cassidy Parker. Three members of the Clanton Gang shot by Wyatt Earp and his posse at the OK Corral: (*left to right*) Tom McLaury, Frank McLaury, and Billy Clanton. Wild Bill Hickock, cowboy, scout, gambler, gunfighter, and part-time lawman. William "Bat" Masterson with the cane he carried all his life, following a wound received in his first gunfight. Wyatt Earp in his mid-twenties.

In the 100 years that had passed since Mexico had overthrown Spanish rule, there had been a succession of wars, coups, and power struggles, but by 1910 Mexico had experienced over 30 years of stability under its strong-arm president, Porfirio Diaz. That was about to come to an end. In the election of 1910, Diaz declared himself the winner by an almost unanimous vote. It was a blatant fraud, which the people did not accept. Riots broke out. Armed insurrection began, and among the many who took up arms were Emilio Zapata ("The Tiger") and José Doroteo Arango Arambula ("The Centaur", better known as Pancho Villa). Both men were champions of the poor – the *peones* and the *campesinos*. Both had a natural genius for the art of warfare. Both achieved lasting fame, becoming the heroes of many books, films, and songs. And both men were to die by assassination.

They were almost exact contemporaries, but came from very different backgrounds. Zapata was the son of an independent *ranchero*, a man never in danger of poverty. Villa, on the other hand, was a poor sharecropper. Zapata had already spent time campaigning for the rights of villagers and the redistribution of land under the slogan "*Tierra y libertad*" ("Land and freedom"). Villa was an outlaw, a man who had become a bandit and cattle rustler after shooting the owner of a *hacienda*, who had raped Villa's young sister.

When the revolution broke out, both men placed themselves in the service of Francisco Madero, one of several candidates for the Mexican presidency. They had immediate success, most famously Villa's victory at the first Battle of Juarez, where his Army of the North inflicted a crushing defeat on the conscript armies of Diaz. Significantly, in the light of what was to come, there was a U.S. presence at the battle, a group of Americans viewing the fighting from the top of railroad boxcars in El Paso.

Emilio Zapata & Pancho Villa

At the height of their fame, Emilio Zapata (*left*) and Pancho Villa sit in adjacent thrones, January 2, 1915.

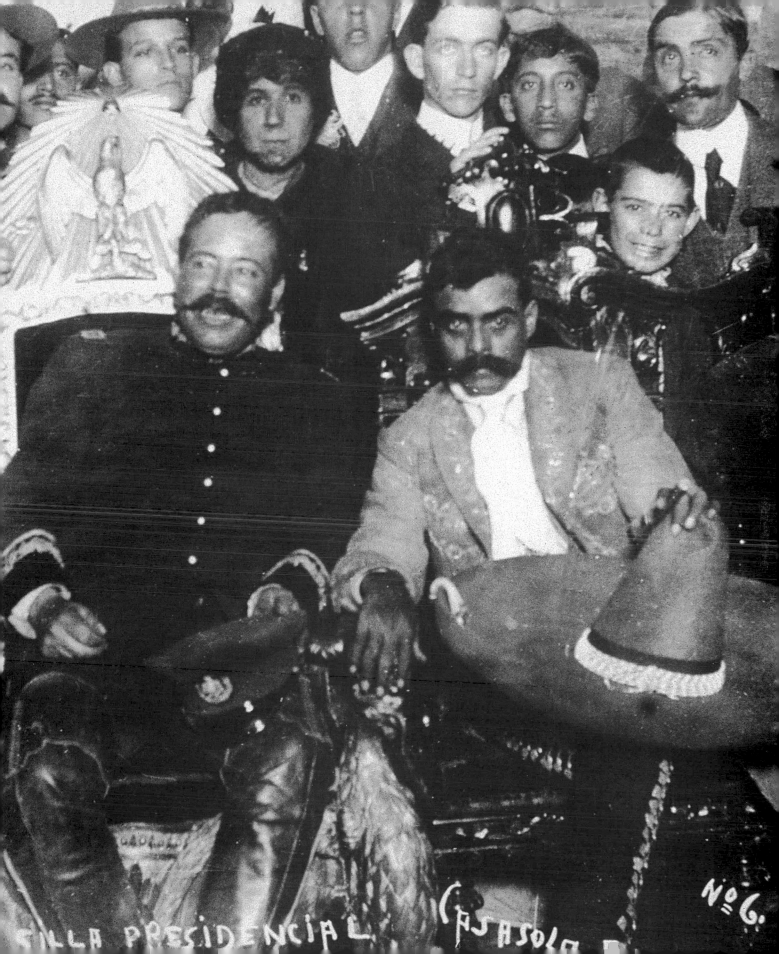

SILLA PRESIDENCIAL CASASOLA N°6

Madero became President, but not for long. In his service was General Victoriano Huerta, a man already conspiring with Felix Diaz (son of the ex-President) and U.S. ambassador Henry Lane Wilson to make himself dictator of Mexico. Huerta crushed a rebellion against Madero, but in 1913 proclaimed himself President, ordered the assassination of Madero, and put an end to all land reforms. Zapata and Villa now took up the cause of another presidential candidate, Venustiano Carranza.

This was beginning of the golden age of Zapata and Villa. Widely acclaimed as champions of the poor, and with the ranks of their separate armies swelled with angry peasants, their exploits were celebrated at home and abroad. It was

(*top*) Pancho Villa, on white horse, and his followers, c.1914. (*left*) Emilio Zapata at the time of the agrarian uprising in South Mexico, 1913. (*right*) A street execution carried out by followers of Venustiano Carranza, 1915.

the last summer of the age of cavalry. Mounted on fine horses, the well-armed *bandolieros* achieved the status of latter-day Robin Hoods, stealing from the rich to give to the poor. Woodrow Wilson, newly elected President of the United States, dismissed Ambassador Wilson, and took up the cause of Carranza, halting the supply of foreign arms and ammunition to Huerta by blockading the port of Vera Cruz. While Zapata controlled the south, Villa won a series of battles at Ciudad Juarez, Tierra Blanca, Chihuahua, and Ojinaga. In December 1914 Zapata and Villa met for the first time and made their historic entry into Mexico City. The following year, Carranza was recognized as President of Mexico by the United States and several Latin American countries. Huerta left Mexico and went into exile on July 14, 1914.

Out of success came splits and recriminations between Carranza and his two great generals. For a while Wilson continued to support Villa, but the *Villistas* suffered defeats. In 1916 Villa led his men into New Mexico, attacking the town of Columbus and killing 10 American soldiers and eight civilians. With Carranza's approval, Wilson sent an army of 11,000 men under General Pershing across the border into Mexico to hunt down Villa. They never succeeded in finding him, and the U.S. troops were withdrawn in 1917, when they were needed on the battlefields of Europe.

Zapata survived another five years before being lured into an ambush by Colonel Jesus Guajardo. The Colonel had intimated that he wished to join Zapata's revolutionaries, but when Zapata arrived at the meeting place, he was gunned down. Villa went into semi-retirement and survived until 1923, when he was assassinated while sitting in his car in Parral, Chihuahua.

American intervention... (*top*) General John Pershing leads his cavalry in pursuit of Pancho Villa, 1916. (*above*) The U.S. Navy prepares to bombard Vera Cruz, 1914. (*opposite*) The Stars and Stripes flies over the Terminal Hotel, Vera Cruz, headquarters of Rear Admiral Frank Fletcher during the Mexican Civil War, 1914.

J ohn Dillinger was a good-looking guy, a ladies' man with a smile not unlike that of Frank Sinatra. Unlike Frank, however, Dillinger neither drank nor smoked, and claimed that his one bad habit was robbing banks – a habit he picked up late in his short life. He was the archetypal American gangster of the 1930s – fearless, ruthless, always with a broad on one arm and a Tommy-gun tucked under the other.

Although he had been a rebellious youth, it was not until he deserted from the U.S. Navy that Dillinger turned to crime. In September 1924 he stole $555 from a local grocer in his hometown of Mooresville. He was arrested, convicted, and sent to Michigan City State Prison for the next eight years. He was released on parole in May 1933, and spent the rest of his life on the run. The desperate spree began when Dillinger and two ex-cons named John Hamilton and Harry Pierpont robbed a number of banks in Indiana and Ohio. Dillinger was caught, but Hamilton and Pierpont broke into the jail where he was held and freed him. The three men then broke into two Indiana police stations to obtain fresh supplies of guns and bullet-proof vests.

For three months, the robberies continued, but big trouble started in January 1934 when Dillinger killed a policeman during a bank raid in East Chicago. He had hit the big time. The posters were up all over the States. Dillinger was Public Enemy Number One. He was recognized and arrested in Tucson, Arizona, and given a 20-year sentence. Just two weeks later, however, he escaped from jail, forcing the guards to back off by brandishing a wooden pistol he had hand-carved and smeared with boot polish.

He tried to disguise his good looks, growing a moustache and having a face lift. He also bathed his fingertips in acid to destroy his fingerprints. The raiding and the killing continued. Acting on a

John Dillinger

"Public Enemy Number One" – the notorious killer and bank robber John Dillinger, a photograph taken when he was on the run.

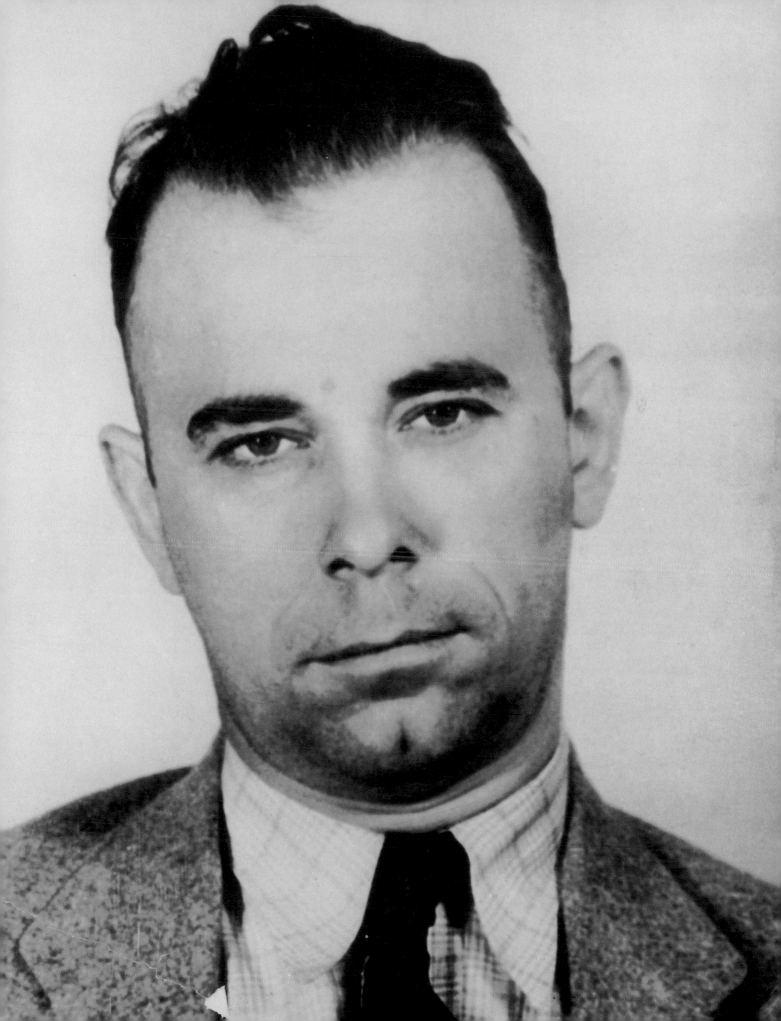

tip from the wife of Dillinger's landlord, on March 31, 1934, the police in St. Paul, Minnesota set up an ambush, but Dillinger and two accomplices managed to shoot their way out. On April 23 Dillinger escaped two more posses, killing two policemen and wounding five others. The end was very near.

Chicago police persuaded a prostitute named Anna Sage to befriend Dillinger. On the night of July 22, 1934, Dillinger and Sage went to a movie theater to see Clark Gable play the part of a gangster in a film called *Manhattan Melodrama*. Sage wore a bright red dress, so that she would be clearly recognized by the police waiting outside. As Dillinger came out, one of the cops called his name – "John!" Dillinger turned and was gunned down in a hail of bullets. At the time, he was wanted for 16 murders.

(*clockwise from above*) An unhappy eight-year-old Dillinger on his father's Indiana farm. A Boy Scout truck in Dillinger country, Wisconsin, at a time when police and law agents were as trigger-happy as the gunmen they pursued, April 26, 1934. Dillinger is handcuffed to Deputy Police Chief Carroll Holby, with defense attorney Joseph Ryan on Dillinger's left, Crown Point, Indiana, February 5, 1934. The FBI poster on Dillinger in June 1934, a month before he was gunned down by police in Chicago.

In the early 1930s, hoodlums and bank-robbers, gunmen and gangsters acquired celebrity status. In the poorer parts of the United States, where the Depression had hit hardest, the exploits of such men as "Pretty Boy" Floyd, Frank "Jelly" Nash, "Machine-Gun" Kelly, Alvin "Creepy" Karvis, and Ma Barker and her gang filled the newspaper front pages, brightened the drab lives of the dirt-farmers and sharecroppers, hobos and migrant workers. Some of the gangsters were seen as modern day Robin Hoods, although very few of them indeed stole from the rich to give to the poor. The attraction was that "Legs" Diamond, "Baby Face" Nelson, Paula "Fat Witted" Harman and a dozen others hit the headlines and gave a buzz to life.

It was also the era of the young Federal Bureau of Investigation, of the G-Men (who were given that name by "Machine Gun" Kelly – or so it is said), and of the "Public Enemy Number 1" who topped the nation's list of wanted men and women in much the same way as a band or singer tops the charts today. The battle between law-enforcement and serious crime was personal, with insults traded at a distance between the head of the FBI, J. Edgar Hoover, and whoever was considered Villain of the Month, like boxers at the weigh-in before a fight.

The criminals themselves were larger than life, colorful characters, who managed to break jail, avoid capture, slip through the net with astonishing ease. They also led charmed lives – for a while. "Legs" Diamond survived so many bullets in him – five in one night from Dutch Schultz's boys – and so many attempts on his life between 1919 and 1931 (when he was finally gunned down by rivals in Albany, New York) that he was nicknamed "The Clay Pigeon of the Underworld".

They were also boastful buccaneers. "Machine Gun" Kelly claimed, erroneously, that the brand new prison built on the island of Alcatraz especially for the likes of him, would never hold him. It

The Era of the Gunman

An impressive and macabre sample of guns and artifacts taken from the collection of Fred and Ma Barker.

WANTED

LESTER M. GILLIS,

aliases GEORGE NELSON, "BABY FACE" NELSON, ALEX GILLIS, LESTER GILES,
"BIG GEORGE" NELSON, "JIMMIE", "JIMMY" WILLIAMS .

On June 23, 1934, HOMER S. CUMMINGS, Attorney General of the United States, under the authority vested in him by an Act of Congress approved June 6, 1934, offered a reward of

$5,000.00
$2,500.00

for information leading to the arrest of Lester M. Gillis.

DESCRIPTION

Age, 25 years; Height, 5 feet 4-3/4 inches; Weight, 133 pounds; Build, medium; Eyes, yellow and grey slate; Hair, light chestnut; Complexion, light; Occupation, oiler.

All claims to any of the aforesaid rewards and all questions and disputes that may arise as among claimants to the foregoing rewards shall be passed upon by the Attorney General and his decisions shall be final and conclusive. The right is reserved to divide and allocate portions of any of said rewards as between several claimants. No part of the aforesaid rewards shall be paid to any official or employee of the Department of Justice.

If you are in possession of any information concerning the whereabouts of Lester M. Gillis, communicate immediately by telephone or telegraph collect to the nearest office of the Division of Investigation, United States Department of Justice, the local offices of which are set forth on the reverse side of this notice.

The apprehension of Lester M. Gillis is sought in connection with the murder of Special Agent W. C. Baum of the Division of Investigation near Rhinelander, Wisconsin on April 23, 1934.

JOHN EDGAR HOOVER, DIRECTOR,
DIVISION OF INVESTIGATION,
UNITED STATES DEPARTMENT OF JUSTICE,
WASHINGTON, D. C.

June 25, 1934

did, for 17 years. Lester M. Gillis – much better known as "Baby Face" Nelson – claimed that he had robbed a bank a day for an entire month, simply to outdo John Dillinger. "Pretty Boy" Floyd – who was given the nickname he hated by Beulah Baird Ash, the madam of a Kansas City brothel – vowed he would never go to prison again after serving his first term. He kept his vow, leaping from a moving train en route to the State Penitentiary, and preferring to be mown down by a hail of bullets in an Ohio field than to be captured alive. Such was his fame, 10,000 people filed past his body in the Sturgis Funeral Home, East Liverpool on the evening of his death, at the rate of 50 a minute, and 20,000 attended his funeral.

(above, left to right) WANTED poster of 1934 for Lester M. Gillis, better known as "Baby Face" Nelson. Arizona Donnie Clark Barker, matriarch of crime, in 1930. *(left)* Charles "Pretty Boy" Floyd with two of his admirers. *(opposite)* Jack "Legs" Diamond, complete with handcuffs, in 1931 – he would have done better to stay in custody.

It was a bumpy ride while it lasted. Clyde Champion Barrow and Bonnie Parker first met in January 1930. Just over four years later they died in an early morning hail of bullets from police and Texas Rangers on a highway near Sailes, Louisiana. In those intervening four years, they had killed 13 people, committed a series of robberies, and assisted in a couple of jail-breaks. Clyde's brother Buck died in custody after a shootout at Platte City, Missouri; his sister-in-law was blinded in the same shootout; and Bonnie was severely burnt and crippled in an automobile wreck.

They were young. When they met, Clyde was 21 and unmarried, and Bonnie was just 19, married to an imprisoned murderer. A month later, Clyde was in jail for robbery, but Bonnie smuggled a gun into him and he escaped. Recaptured almost immediately, Clyde spent the next two years in prison. He was released in February 1932 and the killing started. The first victim was a storeowner in Hillsboro, gunned down as they robbed the store. From then on, they were trigger-happy, killing anyone that got in their way. In all this mayhem, they seemed to have charmed lives, surviving at least two ambushes – one in Iowa (July 1933), another on a highway near Grand Prairie, Texas (November 1933).

That same year, however, the FBI became involved, simply because Bonnie and Clyde had been identified as responsible for the interstate transportation of two stolen automobiles. The luck of then outlaws changed. On May 22, 1934, their pursuers learned that they were due to return to Black Lake, Louisiana the following day. A third ambush was set up. Bonnie and Clyde were killed instantly. Clyde was 25. Bonnie was 23.

On the headstone of Bonnie's grave in the Crown Hill Cemetery, Dallas, the inscription reads: "As the flowers are all made sweeter by the sunshine and the dew, so this old world is made brighter by the lives of folks like you". Storeowners, the Louisiana and Texas police and the FBI may not have agreed with the sentiment.

Bonnie and Clyde

Bonnie Parker and Clyde Barrow poke fun at death and violence in 1932. Two years later death and violence had the last laugh.

On the night of September 4, 1972 eight masked terrorists entered the Israeli quarters at the Olympic Village in Munich. They were members of the Black September Organization (BSO), dedicated to the Palestinian cause and to the overthrow of King Hussein of Jordan. Two members of the Israeli team, Yossef Gutfreund and Yossef Romano, strongly resisted the BSO terrorists, protecting other Israeli athletes and fighting back. Eventually both were killed. Nevertheless, the terrorists were able to take nine hostages.

The terrorists then made their demands – that 234 Palestinians and non-Arabs should be released from jails in Egypt and given safe passage out of that country. They also wanted the German authorities to release Andreas Baader and Ulrike Meinhof, then in jail for crimes committed by the Red Army Faction. The German authorities refused, but offered unlimited money instead. This was turned down by the terrorists, who replied "money means nothing to us, our lives mean nothing to us".

The morning of September 5 passed in unsuccessful negotiations between the terrorists and the Munich police chief and the head of the Egyptian Olympic team. Late in the day, the terrorists demanded transportation to Cairo. At 10:10 P.M., two helicopters took both terrorists and hostages to the nearby Fürstenfeldbrück airbase, where two members of Mossad, German police, and five German snipers were waiting. None of the snipers was equipped with telescopic sights or night-vision scopes, and none had received special training. On the airbase runway was a Boeing 727 with a handful of armed German police inside, disguised as flight crew. The plan was that these men would deal with the terrorists from the first helicopter, while the snipers took out those from the second, but at the last minute, the German police on board the 727 aborted their mission.

Black September

The chilling image of one of the Black September gang members in the Olympic Village, Munich, September 7, 1972.

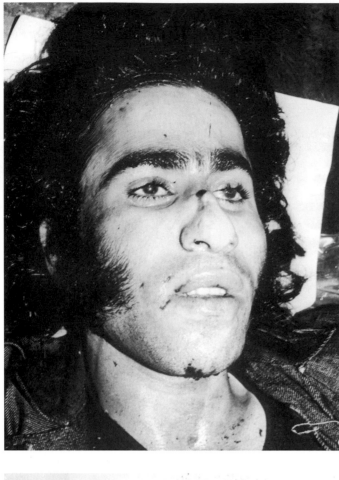

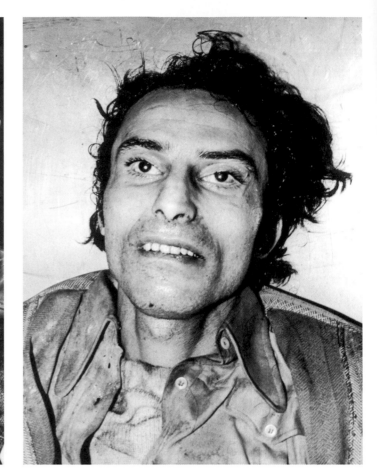

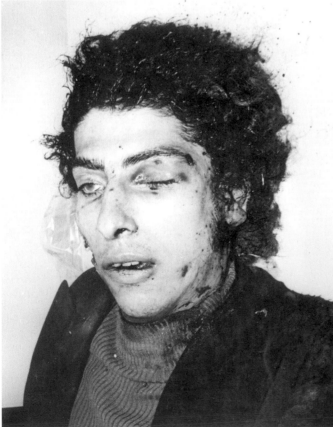

The helicopters touched down at 10:30 P.M. Four of the BSO terrorists held the pilots at gunpoint. Two others boarded the 727. Finding it empty, they knew that they had been tricked and that there was no deal. Almost at once, the German authorities ordered the snipers to open fire. There was immediate chaos. Two of the terrorists were killed, but others scrambled to safety and returned fire. The helicopters' pilots fled, but the hostages were tied up and could not move from the helicopters. In the confusion German police fired on their own snipers, seriously wounding one, while others attempted to continue negotiations. At 0:06 A.M. on September 6, the terrorists began killing their hostages. In all 17 people died – 11 members of the Israeli team, one German policeman, and five of the terrorists.

Avery Brundage, President of the International Olympic Committee, made no reference to the massacre when he later made a speech praising the strength of the Olympic movement.

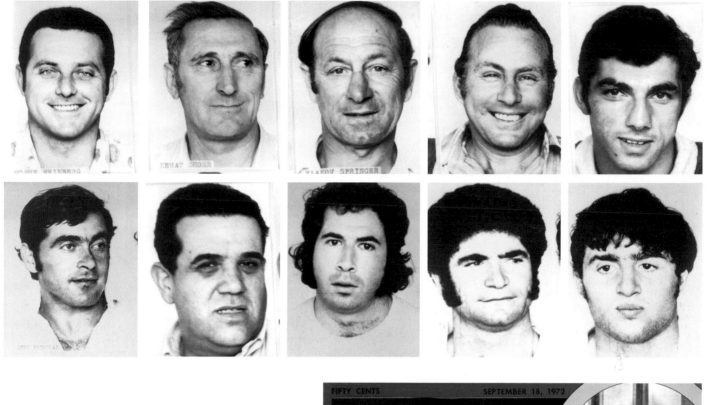

(*opposite*) Three of the Palestinian terrorists. (*above, top row, left to right*) The victims: Moshe Weinberg, Kehat Schur, Yakov Springer, Amitzur Shapira, and Eliezaar Halfen. (*bottom row, left to right*) Zeev Friedman, Yossef Gutfreund, David Berger, Yosef Romano, and Mark Slavin. (*right*) *Time* magazine cover for September 18, 1972.

The year 1968 was one of the most disturbed and turbulent years in American history. It saw the assassinations of Martin Luther King Jnr. and Bobby Kennedy, rioting in the streets of 125 cities, anti-Vietnam War protest reaching an all-time high along with demands for social and political change. It also saw a great deal of advance publicity for a planned Festival of Life that promised major disruption of the Democratic National Convention in Chicago.

Trouble began there on August 24 when police clashed with demonstrators who had been denied the right to sleep in public parks, and continued with an escalation of violence for the next four days. When the Convention opened on August 28, the eight leaders of the protest movement (Abbie Hoffman, Jerry Rubin, David Dellinger, Tom Hayden, Rennie Davies, John Froines, Lee Weiner, and Bobby Searle) were arrested. Thirteen months later, they were put on trial, charged with rioting and incitement to riot. The jurors selected were not favorably disposed toward the Chicago Eight, one expressing the view that they "should have been shot down by the police". The attitude of the Eight in court did not help their cause, for they cracked jokes, slept, and on one occasion smoked marijuana.

Attitudes hardened during the trial, with Bobby Searle calling the judge a "Fascist dog and a racist". These particular charges may not have been valid, but Judge Hoffman's stance was certainly not impartial. He began sentencing the defendants for contempt long before the jury had finished its deliberations. These convictions were all later reversed on appeal.

Five of the Eight were found guilty, fined $5,000 each and sentenced to five years imprisonment, but three years later the Seventh Circuit Court of Appeals reversed all convictions, citing Judge Hoffman's antagonistic attitude. The Court also noted that the FBI, with the Judge's knowledge, had bugged the offices of the defense attorneys.

Chicago Eight

Seven members of the Chicago Eight (without ties) in October 1969: (*left to right*) Jerry Rubin, David Dellinger, Lee Weiner, John Froines, Tom Hayden, Rennie Davis, and Abbie Hoffman

KIDNAPPED

Ill-Gotten Gains

Arrested narcotic dealers appear at the Federal
Building in Chicago on March 1, 1954.

He was known as "Slick Willie" because he was an immaculate dresser – few crooks have ever taken such trouble over their appearance. He was born in 1901 in the Irish-American district of Brooklyn, finished with school at the age of 12, and in his 79 years of life his longest period of legitimate employment lasted only 18 months.

Slick Willie Sutton's speciality was robbing banks – he hit about 100 of them between the late 1920s and his final arrest in 1952. Why asked why he chose to rob banks, Sutton's simple answer was "because that's where the money is". He often worked alone, arming himself with a pistol or sub-machine gun, for, as he said, "You can't rob a bank on charm and personality". He liked to disguise himself as some minor official, a mailman, police officer, maintenance man, or postal telegraph messenger, and made a habit of arriving at banks or stores that he intended to rob shortly before they opened. He was always polite. A witness to one of his bank raids described the scene as like being at the movies, except that the usher had a gun.

The Corn Exchange Bank and Trust Company in Philadelphia ended his criminal career. His first attempt to rob it was made in February 1933, but was thwarted by a passer-by. His second attempt the following year was successful at first, but a month later he was arrested. Sutton was sentenced to serve 25 to 50 years, subsequently increased to 105 years. Then, 10 years into his sentence he escaped but was recaptured the same day. A more successful attempt was made on February 10, 1947. Dressed as a guard, Sutton carried a ladder across the prison yard. When the searchlights hit him, he called out "It's OK", and strolled out of the Eastern State Penitentiary. He was finally released for reasons of ill health in 1969, and died in Florida in 1980.

Willie Sutton

Immaculate as always, Willie Sutton awaits trial in a
Brooklyn court house in May 1952.

On August 8, 1963, on a quiet stretch of line in Bedfordshire, the Glasgow to London "up-postal" train was robbed of over £2.5 million ($5 million). It was one of the most audacious crimes in British history. Bruce Reynolds, a London antique dealer and accomplished thief, recruited a team of 15 men for the job, including a railroad expert, a train driver, and an expert electrician. He negotiated the purchase of Leatherslade Farm as hideout 27 miles from the site of the planned robbery, and stole army uniforms, an army lorry, and two Land Rovers.

The planning was meticulous, the execution faultless. Just after midnight, disguised as an army team on manoeuvres, the gang left the isolated farm and drove to Bridego Bridge. At 3:00 A.M., Roger Cordrey, the electrician, and another member of the gang activated false signals, bringing the mail train to a halt at Sears Crossing. The train was split and, since the gang's own driver was unable to release the vacuum brake, Jack Mills, the real train driver, was forced to shunt the locomotive and the first two coaches to Bridego Bridge, where the rest of the gang waited. The postal workers in the mail coach were gagged, bound and left lying face-down on the floor of the coach. The gang then formed a human chain down the embankment to the waiting lorry. Just forty minutes from the time the train had been stopped, Reynolds and his men made their getaway back to Leatherslade Farm.

The police responded quickly. From their radio, the gang learnt that the police knew an army vehicle had been involved in the robbery and suspected that those responsible were holed up in a local farmhouse. One of the gang, Buster Edwards, suggested that they burn the farm to the ground – to avoid leaving fingerprints or other evidence. The idea was rejected. Smoke and flames in high summer might attract unwelcome attention, and, anyway, someone had been paid to "sanitize" the farmhouse the moment they left.

Great Train Robbery

An aerial photograph of the site of what was then the greatest train robbery in the history of British crime – the line from Cheddington Station to Bridego Bridge, August 1963.

WHERE THE RAIDERS STRUCK
E ROBBED
AIL TRAIN
CHEDDINGTON STATION

That "someone" did nothing, and when police raided the farm they discovered fingerprints of everyone involved – on beer bottles, ketchup bottles and on pieces of a Monopoly set the gang had played with to while away the hours. One by one, the gang were arrested – Cordrey, Charles Wilson, James White, Tommy Wisbey, James Hussey, Robert Welch, Reynolds, Edwards, Gordon Goody, Brian Field, William Boal, Leonard Field, and Ronald Biggs. All received lengthy jail sentences.

Biggs, alone of the gang, achieved folk-hero status. This was largely as a result of his escape from prison on July 8, 1965, his flight to Australia and then to Brazil, and his subsequent battle to stay out of the hands of the British police over a period of 37 years before giving himself up on May 7, 2001.

(*opposite top row*) Three of the robbers: James White, Charles Wilson, and Bruce Reynolds. (*middle row*) Ronnie Biggs; the train driver, Jack Mills, with is head bandaged shortly after the robbery. (*opposite below*) Three of the suspects arrested in connection with the "Great Train Robbery" leaving Linslade Court with blankets over their heads on August 16, 1963. (*above*) Banknotes hidden in the walls of the caravan of James White. The police found £35,000 ($70,000) here.

When stock markets are manipulated by insider trading, innocent people will almost always lose money, and the money they have lost simply ceases to exist. It cannot be handed back. If a member of the public buys stock at $10 a share, and the value of that stock falls by 10 percent, then not only has that person lost a dollar a share, that dollar has disappeared. And if the value of the stock falls by over 90 percent, as it did in the case of the Enron Corporation, then some people may lose almost all they own.

When the crash came for Enron in December 2001, investors lost some $60 billion, the firm's accounts going back five years had to be rewritten, and Enron filed for bankruptcy. As in the fall of the Roman Empire, too many people had been having too good a time to see what was coming, which is all it takes for others to hasten and worsen the collapse by adding a little mischief of their own. Long before the courts of law had found anyone guilty in the Enron affair, the court of public opinion had tried and condemned certain parties – notably the accounting firm of Arthur Andersen. As papers were hurriedly shredded and files destroyed, one expert pronounced the last rites on Andersen: "The verdict doesn't matter any more. Arthur Andersen is dead. Once the indictment was handed down, clients started jumping faster than they did off the *Titanic*." Or indeed than they did from the windows of Wall Street back in 1929.

In court the top echelon of Enron cut sorry figures. Kenneth Lay, former Chair of Enron, asserted that the collapse was primarily the fault of the *Wall Street Journal* for publishing articles that had "kicked off a run on the bank". He might perhaps more justifiably have blamed one particular journalist – Bethany McLean, whose 2001 article in the ironically-named magazine *Fortune* first suggested that the company was overvalued. It was her persistence that ultimately led to the "smartest guys in the room" looking so silly in court. Lay died of a heart attack on July 5, 2006 three months before his scheduled sentencing.

Enron

(*top left*) Enron Headquarters in downton Houston, Texas, August 13, 1999. "The Smartest Guys in the Room": (*top right*) Andrew Fastow, former Chief Financial Officer; (*bottom left*) Ken Lay, former CEO; and (*bottom right*) David B. Duncan, former Arthur Andersen accountant.

1400 Smith Street

Miscarriages of Justice?

Gerry Conlon squats beside the grave of his father, Guiseppe.
Conlon spent 15 years in prison falsely accused, along with his
father, of a series of pub bombings in England in 1974. His
father died in prison.

Thursday, August 4, 1892, was a boiling hot day in Fall River, Massachusetts. Generations of schoolchildren have been certain they knew what happened in the Bordens' comfortable home at 92 Second Street that day:

Lizzie Borden took an axe
And gave her mother forty whacks.
When she saw what she had done,
She gave her father forty-one.

The law was not so sure. It was beyond all doubt that somebody had killed Andrew and Abby Borden, Lizzie's father and stepmother. There they were – Mr. Borden with his face cut by eleven blows, one eye cut in half, and his nose severed – Mrs. Borden struck down by 19 blows, the blood on her body dark and congealing swiftly in the heat.

Six days after the killings, Lizzie Borden was charged with murder. She pleaded "not guilty". Ten months later her trial began. The prosecution believed that they had found a motive for Lizzie to murder her father and stepmother. Shortly before his death, Andrew Borden had made a new will leaving $25,000 each to Lizzie and her sister Emma, but $500,000 to Abby Borden, his wife. There were rumors that Lizzie had been trying to buy prussic acid from a local shop, that the elder Bordens believed someone was trying to poison them. Perhaps Lizzie could not wait for the death of both father and stepmother before she could inherit her share of the fortune.

The jury did not agree. It took them just over an hour to find Lizzie not guilty on all charges. She left the court a free woman, although the rest of her life she was ostracized by most of Fall River society. Until she died in 1927, Lizzie had to live in the shadow of the suspicion that the jury had got it wrong, the song had got it right.

Lizzie Borden

The bedroom where the axe murders took place, now converted into a Lizzie Borden museum and guestroom by the owner, Martha McGinn.

Margaretha Geertruida Zelle was born in the Netherlands in 1876. As a young woman she went to live in Java, where she learnt something of Oriental dancing and entered into an unsuccessful marriage with a Dutch naval officer. With her liking for men of power and her developing talents as an exotic dancer, it was natural that she should make her way to Paris, and here she earned her living as courtesan, artists' model and dancer, changing her name to Mata Hari – Indonesian for "Eye of the Day". She was not classically beautiful, but she was attractive and decidedly arousing. She made friends, and also enemies – for she gained a reputation as a wanton and promiscuous woman.

As a citizen of the neutral Netherlands, Mata Hari traveled with relative freedom during World War I, moving between France and Germany via Spain and England. She told the British that she was a French agent, but the French authorities never supported this story. Then in January 1917, the German military attaché in Madrid transmitted messages to Berlin praising the activities of a spy with the code-name H-21. The messages were intercepted, and since they were transmitted in a code which the Germans knew had been broken, the French were able to read them and identify H-21 as Mata Hari.

On February 13, 1917 she was arrested in her Paris hotel room. She was put on trial, accused among other things of being responsible for the deaths of tens of thousands of French soldiers. She was found guilty and sentenced to death by firing squad.

Romantic legends clothe her execution. She is said to have blown a kiss to her executioners, to have flung open her coat and revealed her naked body, to have murmured as her last words "Merci, monsieur". There is even a story, reminiscent of Puccini's *Tosca*, that the firing squad had been bribed to use blanks. What is known is that she was shot on October 15, 1917.

Mata Hari

A discreetly dressed Mata Hari on the day of her arrest for spying, 1917.

On May 5, 1920 Nicola Sacco and Bartolemeo Vanzetti were arrested and charged with the murder of two payroll guards during an armed robbery at South Braintree, Massachusetts. Vanzetti had already been charged with an earlier attempted robbery at Bridgewater, and prior to his trial with Sacco was sentenced to serve 10 to 15 years for this crime.

The case of Sacco and Vanzetti has to be seen in the context of the Red Scare of 1919 to 1920. Revolution in Europe had excited workers and anarchists in America, and at the same time horrified employers and conservatives. Anarchist violence, which included an attempt on the life of the U.S. Attorney-General, met with police brutality. Congress voted funds to launch the career of a young man named J. Edgar Hoover, whose first assignment was the Sacco and Vanzetti case.

The two Italians were humble men – Sacco was a shoe-maker and Vanzetti a fish-seller – but they were known to be ardent supporters of *Cronaca Sovversiva*, a highly-influential Italian-language anarchist journal. Defense counsel Fred H. Moore, a well-known socialist lawyer, admitted this much, seeking to turn the trial into a political battle. He got what he wanted, but had underestimated the intensity of feeling that stormed into the courtroom. Judge Webster Thayer was not impressed. He described the defendants as "those anarchist bastards". When the jury returned a verdict of "guilty", it was hardly surprising.

There were protests against the conduct of the trial throughout the world. Intellectuals and academics lined up to continue the struggle on Sacco and Vanzetti's behalf. It lasted a further six years until, on April 9, 1927, the two men were sentenced to death. They were executed four months later, by which time they had ceased to be mere men, but had become symbols to many of all that is best in the world, and to others of all that is worst.

Sacco and Vanzetti

Bartolomeo Vanzetti (centre) and Nicola Sacco (right) sit handcuffed to each other in police custody at Dedham, Massachusetts, following their arrest in 1921.

In 1925 a mine-owner named George Rappleyea persuaded a group of his fellow business-men in Dayton, Tennessee that their small town would gain considerable publicity if they could find a local teacher ready to take on the Tennessee General Assembly. The Assembly had recently passed the Butler Act, which declared that it was illegal for anyone to teach "any theory that denies the story of the Divine Creation of man as taught in the Bible, and to teach instead that man has descended from a lower order of animals."

They found their teacher in 24-year-old John T. Scopes, the Rhea County High School's football coach who had taught the occasional science class. They also found both prosecution and defense attorneys for their show trial, but as news of the case spread, an alternative, all-star cast gathered. William Jennings Bryan, three-time Democratic presidential candidate and avowed fundamentalist, joined the prosecution. Clarence Darrow, a lawyer known throughout the States for his brilliant defense of Leopold and Loeb, volunteered his services to Scopes.

The first trial was a sensation. Bryan and Darrow were bitterly opposed over the issue, although they had much respect for each other. Bryan had recently published a book called *In His Image*, which argued that the doctrine of evolution was both irrational and immoral. Darrow was an avowed agnostic. Pitted against each other, they pulled out all the stops, and national interest in the trial – the first to be broadcast on radio in the United States – was huge.

It was another member of the defense team, Dudley Field Malone, who raised the roof of the little courtroom. Bryan had declared a "duel to the death with evolution". Malone claimed that there could never be "a duel with the truth". The case developed into a passionate debate between Darrow and Bryan, fighting respectively for science and religion. Ironically, Bryan cited

Scopes Trial

The humble high school teacher whose trial shook an entire nation – John T. Scopes of Tennessee in 1932.

the case of Leopold and Loeb, quoting the very words and arguments that Darrow had used in that trial, and scorning the notion that evolution could somehow be used as an excuse for the evil that men did.

When Scopes was found guilty and fined $100, Bryan offered to pay the fine, but the case went to appeal. The complicated arguments put forward by Scopes's team were of no avail, but the Appeal Court set aside the conviction on the grounds that it was not in the original judge's power to impose a fine of more than $50.

The argument raged on and on, as it does today. It was never resolved, but the businessmen of Dayton did succeed in gaining international fame for their town.

(*top*) Friends at large, foes in the courtroom – Clarence Darrow (left) and William Jennings Bryan (right) in the courtroom during the "Monkey Trial" at South Dayton, July 1925. (*opposite*) Darrow, with arms folded, casts doubt on the literal interpretation of the Bible during the trial. Those attending the trial found much to entertain and outrage them.

Between 1884 and 1930 there were 3,724 recorded incidents of lynching in the United States, an average of over 80 a year. These figures are almost certainly an underestimation. The vast majority of the victims were African Americans, the vast majority of those who did the killing were white. The battle to end this barbaric practice has been long and hard. Back in 1884, in Memphis, a black woman named Ida Wells, editor of a newspaper called *Free Speech*, reported that in a short period 728 blacks had been lynched by white mobs, over two-thirds of them grabbed off the streets or snatched from their homes for petty offences such as shoplifting or being drunk in public. A white mob then attacked her office and smashed the printing press. Luckily for her, Ida Wells was out of town at the time.

Many hoped that the election of Franklin D. Roosevelt to the Presidency in 1932 would end lynching. A bill was presented to Congress in 1935, but Roosevelt refused to back it, claiming that white voters in the South would never forgive him if he made lynching illegal. Opinions hardened after the lynching that year of a young black named Rubin Stacy. Six deputies were escorting Stacy to Dade County Jail in Miami, when he was snatched from them by a mob, and taken to the home of a woman who had made a complaint against him. Here, in front of a large crowd of men, women and children, he was hanged from a tree. A subsequent investigation revealed that Stacy, a homeless tenant farmer, had gone to the house to ask for food.

Two years after Roosevelt's death, the singer Paul Robeson made a speech against lynching at Madison Square Garden: "Stop the lynchers! What about it, President Truman? Why have you failed to speak out against this evil?" Like his predecessor, Truman did nothing.

Lynchings

The lynching of 18-year-old Tom Shipp and
19-year-old Abe Smith, Indiana, August 7, 1930.
Not one of the mob was charged.

The crime was horrendous, but the case is remembered not for the crime, but for the punishment. Rainey Bethea was hanged in front of a crowd of 15,000 people in Owensboro, Kentucky, on August 14, 1936.

Bethea was a young black who had arrived in Owensboro three years earlier and had already had trouble with the law. In April 1935, he stole two purses from the Vogue Beauty Shop. As their value was over $25, he was convicted of grand larceny and sentenced to a year in the State Penitentiary. On his release, he returned to Owensboro, where he was convicted of being drunk and disorderly a month later. Since he couldn't pay the $100 fine – at the time he was making $7 a week – he was imprisoned for three months. Early on the morning of June 7, 1936, he was drunk again. He broke into the home of Lischia Edwards, entering via her bedroom window. The old lady woke. Bethea strangled her, raped her, and then searched through her jewellery – removing his own black celluloid prison ring as he did so. He took what he wanted, left his own ring, and fled, hiding the jewels in a barn not far away.

When Lischia Edwards' body was discovered, the Coroner was summoned. It was he who found Bethea's ring. A week later Bethea was arrested as he boarded a river barge. To their credit, the police did all they could to prevent him being lynched, for the woman he had killed was white, and local feeling ran high. Bethea made a full confession, but said that he did not know whether his victim was alive when he raped her. This was a significant point, for in Kentucky in 1936 it was not illegal to have intercourse with a corpse. The nature of his crime also posed a problem for the prosecution. The death penalty for murder and robbery was administered by the electric chair; for rape, by hanging. Bethea was tried for rape, and it took the jury less than five minutes to find him guilty.

Last American Public Hanging

The public hanging of Rainey Bethea, August 14, 1936. On the scaffold G. Phil Hanna is placing the noose around Bethea's neck.

The case of Dr. Sam Sheppard became the subject of a highly successful 1960s American TV network drama series called *The Fugitive* and of a later Hollywood movie, both of which offered far happier endings to the story of Sam Sheppard's long fight to prove that he was not guilty of murdering his wife, than real life afforded.

On July 4, 1954 at 5:45 A.M. John Spencer Houk, a friend of the Sheppards, received a telephone call from Sheppard, urging him to come at once and ending "I think they've killed Marilyn!" Houk and his wife arrived at the house in Bay Village, Cleveland about 10 minutes later. They found the house in a mess, indicating that it had been ransacked or burgled. Sheppard was slumped in a chair on the first floor, wet, bruised, groggy, and in pain. Marilyn was in her bedroom, lying in a pool of blood, with her head fractured in a number of places. The police suspected Sheppard from the start. They believed the evidence pointing to a burglary had been fabricated and it seemed he had a motive for killing his wife as he was having an affair with a female colleague at work. Sheppard was arrested, charged and, on December 21, 1954 convicted of the murder of his wife. He was sentenced to life imprisonment.

He repeatedly asserted his innocence and demanded a retrial, but it was not until October 1966 that permission was granted to reopen the case. Certain flaws in the prosecution case now appeared. The police at the time had assumed that Sheppard's own injuries had been self-inflicted, but had made no investigation to discover whether or not this would have been possible. The medical expert who had claimed that a "surgical instrument" had been responsible for Marilyn Sheppard's death, now admitted that he had no certain knowledge that such an instrument existed. This threw enough doubt on the conviction for Sheppard to be acquitted at the retrial and released from prison. But, unlike the happy endings on TV and in the movie, his career was ruined, his two subsequent marriages both failed, and he died on April 6, 1970.

Dr. Sam Sheppard

Wearing a brace, supporting both his neck and his story
that he had been attacked, Dr. Sam Sheppard sits in
court, on trial for the murder of his wife.

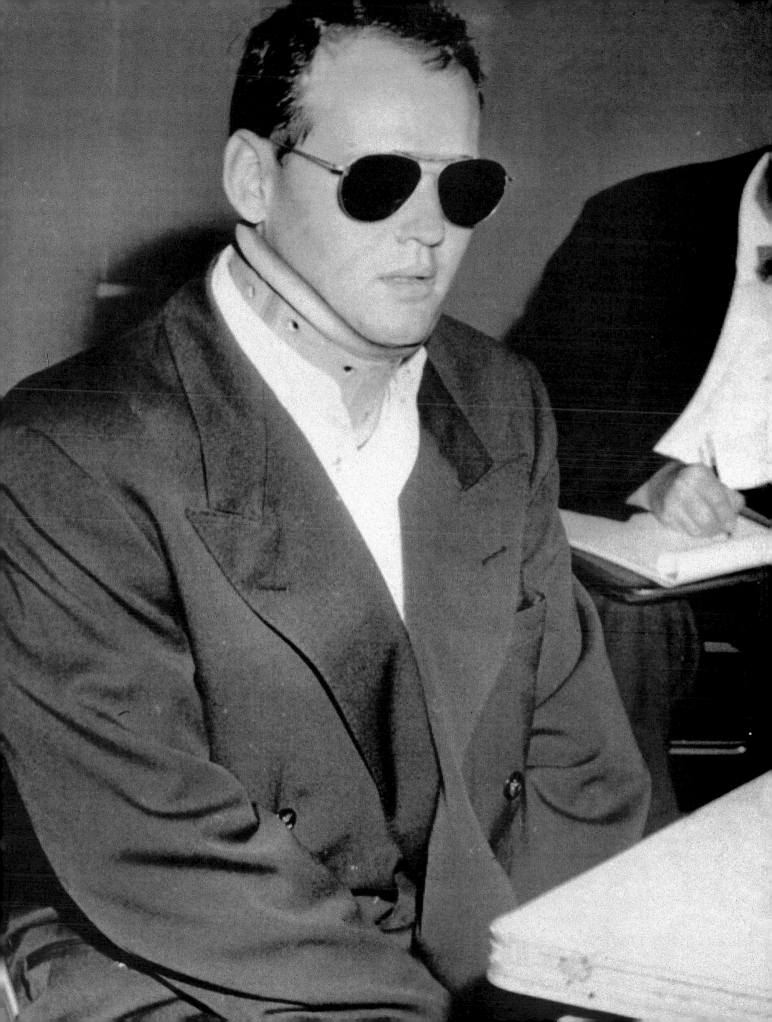

In August 1955, 14-year-old Emmett Till left Chicago to visit his uncle, Mose Wright, near the town of Money in Mississippi. Emmett had experienced race hatred in Chicago, but was unprepared for the strict segregation of the South. When he showed some local boys a picture of a white girl who was one of his friends, one of them dared him to talk to a white woman in a nearby candy store. Emmett took the dare, went into the store and, as he left, called out "Bye, baby" to the woman.

A few nights later, Roy Bryant and J. W. Millam came to Mose Wright's cabin. Bryant was the owner of the store and husband of the woman Emmett had spoken to, Millam was her brother. They took Emmett and drove away. Emmett's body was subsequently found in the Tallahatchie river. There was a bullet in his head, his skull had been crushed, and one of his eyes had been gouged out. Mose Wright identified the body from an initialed ring on one of the fingers.

At first, whites and blacks alike were horrified. Bryant and Millam had already been arrested for the kidnap but no local white lawyer would act for them. Then the case attracted national attention. In Chicago, Emmett's mother insisted on an open-casket funeral, so that "all the world can see what they did to my son". Stark photographs appeared in the black press. Emmett's murder was condemned in black churches throughout the North. Attitudes hardened. Many southerners were incensed by descriptions of their society as being based on "the barbarity of segregation".

Lawyers now stepped forward to defend Bryant and Millam, but there were no witnesses prepared to testify against them. Finally, Mose Wright bravely stepped forward and, in open court, pointed to the two men who had taken his nephew. It made no difference. The defence attorney declared: "I'm sure every last Anglo-Saxon one of you has the courage to free these men in the face of outside pressure". The jury found Bryant and Millam not guilty.

Emmett Till

Roy Bryant (centre left) and J. W. Millam (centre right) pose with their wives following their acquittal on the charge of the murder of Emmett Till, September 1955.

From the very beginning of his political career, Joseph McCarthy showed that he was a man of terrifying determination. His rise was meteoric, as he lied about his war record and smeared his opponents – driving one to suicide. Once elected as a Republican to the Senate, he quickly set about attacking members of the Democratic administration.

The idea of whipping up anti-communist hysteria was given to him in 1950 by a Roman Catholic priest named Edmund Walsh, and McCarthy successfully used the tactic when he stood for re-election to the Senate that year. He also took advantage of national worries about the Korean War to whip up a Red Scare, with investigations into communists quickly turning into witch-hunts. At McCarthy's insistence, 30,000 books allegedly written by communists were purged from American libraries. Academics and lawyers, politicians and commentators were threatened by him, and few of his targets had the courage to fight back. One exception was Hank Greenspun, editor of the *Las Vegas Sun*, who called McCarthy "a sadistic bum" and wrote: "I would hate to see some simpleton get the chair for such a public service as getting rid of McCarthy".

His success went to his head. In 1954 McCarthy turned on the U.S. Army, denouncing senior officers as traitors and Soviet agents. President Eisenhower, who had derived some support from McCarthy during his own presidential campaign, was furious at this step. Opponents tough-ened their resistance to McCarthyism and counter-attacked. In a famous 1954 edition of TV's *See It Now*, Ed Murrow said: "The line between investigating and persecuting is a very fine one and the junior Senator from Wisconsin (McCarthy) has stepped over it repeatedly". Six months later, a censure motion on McCarthy's conduct was passed in the Senate by 67 votes to 22.

McCarthy was an alcoholic, and the end was not far away. He died of acute hepatitis in the Bethesda Naval Hospital on May 2, 1957.

McCarthy Witch-hunts

Senator Joseph McCarthy (left) with lawyer Roy M. Cohn
during the Army Hearings in Washington D.C., 1954.

At first sight, the bodies of the three victims would have suggested that they had nothing in common save their youth – Chaney was 21, Schwerner was 24, Goodman was 20. One was a black Mississippian, one was a Jewish activist, one was from an upper-middle-class New York family. All three were found in an earthen dam on the Old Jolly Farm in Neshoba County, Mississippi, a state described by Martin Luther King Jnr. in his famous "I have a dream…" speech as "sweltering in injustice". They had been shot, and from the state of the bodies the shooting had taken place several weeks earlier. What the three young victims shared, however, was a passionate belief in the U.S. Civil Rights Movement of the 1960s.

On June 21, 1964, they had been preparing for the opening of a Freedom School in a church that had been firebombed by the Ku Klux Klan. Driving back to their office they were arrested by Deputy Sheriff Cecil Price, held for a while, then released when it was dark. A white mob was waiting for them. At 2:00 A.M. Buford Posey, a local member of the NAACP (National Association for the Advancement of Colored People), was called by Edgar Ray Killen, the "chaplain" of the KKK and a part-time preacher. "We took care of your three friends tonight," said Killen, "and you're next." Posey called the FBI.

James Jordan, a Klan member, agreed to co-operate with the FBI. In the belief that no Mississippi jury would convict those responsible for the murders, the FBI decided that the charge would be conspiracy to deprive the three victims of their civil rights. Those charged included Deputy Sheriff Price and Sheriff Lawrence Rainey, both members of the KKK. On October 21, 1967, Jordan and Price were convicted and sentenced to four years and six years respectively. Rainey and Killen were acquitted, one of the jurors saying that there was no way she could convict a preacher.

Mississippi Burning

Members of the Mississippi Freedom Democratic Party hold banners of the slain volunteers, (left to right) Andrew Goodman, James Chaney, and Michael Schwerner.

Another 38 years passed before Edgar Killen was brought to trial. On June 21, 2005 – the 41st anniversary of the killings – the jury returned their verdict on the three charges of murder and manslaughter against him. They found him guilty of the manslaughter of Chaney, Schwerner, and Goodman. Killen was 80 years old at the time of his trial, confined to a wheelchair and breathing oxygen. He remained unrepentant, branding his victims from all those years ago as "Communists", who were threatening Mississippi's way of life.

(*clockwise from opposite top*) The burnt-out station wagon, in which Chaney, Goodman, and Schwerner were last seen alive, dumped in the Bogue Chitto swamp. Investigators uncover remains of the three victims, August 28, 1963. Preacher and former Klansman Edgar Ray Killen at his trial for the murders of the three civil rights workers in June 2005.

On the night of October 30, 1975, a group of teenagers were celebrating Mischief Night in the rich area of the little Connecticut town of Greenwich, known as Belle Haven. Among them was 15-year-old Martha Moxley. It was all innocent fun among the clapboard homes – a few eggs thrown, some pranks played – but when Martha failed to return home at her usual "curfew" hour, her mother grew worried. She persuaded Martha's older brother to cruise the neighborhood looking for his sister. Midnight came and went with no trace of Martha, and it was not until nearly 4:00 A.M. the following morning that the police were called. It took another eight hours before her dead body was found. She had been battered with a golf club and stabbed in the neck.

The Belle Haven police were not used to crime at this level. The initial investigation was clumsily conducted. No police doctor was called. No close-up photographs were taken of the body. Traces of blood on nearby leaves went unnoticed. The probable time of death was not properly investigated. No notice was taken of the stab wound in Martha's neck. Subsequent enquiries showed that Rushton Skakel, a powerful and influential local man – the brother of Ethel Kennedy, Bobby Kennedy's widow – was pulling strings to hinder the investigation, for the most likely suspect was one or other of his two sons, Thomas and Michael.

At first Thomas Skakel was the prime suspect. He was the last person to have been seen with Martha, and he owned a set of golf clubs from which one was now missing. After a while, however, his younger brother Michael was seen by many as the more likely culprit. Michael was a strange boy with a reputation for killing small animals, often with a golf club. He claimed that at the time of the murder he was masturbating in a tree close to Martha's bedroom window. It was not an impressive alibi. Over the next few years, Michael spent a lot of time in special educational institutions for youngsters with behavior difficulties.

Michael Skakel

Michael Skakel is led from court on the first day of his sentencing hearing in Norwalk, Connecticut, August 28, 2002.

Rushton was anxious to prove his boys' innocence. At a cost of several million dollars, he hired a top firm of private investigators to prove that Thomas and Michael were in the clear, then demanded that the results of their investigation be suppressed.

Some 23 years passed before a Grand Jury reopened the case in June 1998, issuing a warrant for the arrest of Michael Skakel. Bail was posted at $500,000. When Michael was found guilty in May 2002 he was sentenced to 20 years to life. His appeal was rejected in January 2006.

(*above*) The "Night of Mischief" victim – Martha Moxley, the 15-year-old victim of a teenage murderer in Belle Haven, 1975. (*opposite*) The Skakel family all at sea in the 1970s, proof that money can't buy happiness. The domineering father, Rushton, is seated, center.

They became known as the Atlanta Child Murders – a series of 29 killings of black teenagers and children that took place between 1979 and 1981. With the exception of one victim who had been raped, the killings appeared to be without motive, and the means of killing included suffocation, strangulation, shooting, and stabbing. The killings came to an end with the arrest of a 23-year-old music promoter and freelance photographer named Wayne Williams.

Williams came to the attention of the police in the early hours of May 22, 1981 when patrolmen near the Chattahoochee River heard a splash and saw a young black man driving away in a station-wagon. They stopped the driver and questioned him, but then let him go. Two days later the body of Nathaniel Cater was found floating in the river, and the driver of the station-wagon, Wayne Williams, was arrested. There was enough evidence against him to charge Williams with murder. He had been seen leaving a theater with Cater shortly before the young man disappeared. Dog hairs on Cater's body matched hair found in Williams's station-wagon and home. Police discovered that Williams had been seen in the company of other murder victims. Williams was charged with a second killing, that of Jimmy Payne.

But the evidence against Williams was largely circumstantial, and the police were unable to come up with a convincing motive. Although Williams was charged with just two killings, the prosecution at his trial was allowed to bring in evidence relating to the other 27 murders. Williams was found guilty of both murders and sentenced to two consecutive terms of life imprisonment. The Atlanta Police declared that another 20 of the 29 murders had been solved.

Not everyone was satisfied that justice had been done. On May 6, 2005 the DeKalb County Police Chief Louis Graham ordered the re-opening of four cases where the killings had been attributed to Williams. The authorities in neighboring Fulton County, where most of the killings took place, did not respond. Williams has always denied being responsible for the killings.

Wayne Williams

Wayne Williams is taken to his pretrial hearing, charged with the murder of two young men from Atlanta, October 20, 1981.

It played like a soap opera. For months the most compelling viewing on television was the
O. J. Simpson show. The images of bloodstained bodies, of the fugitive batting along the
freeway with scores of police cars in hot pursuit, and the ensuing courtroom drama had all
America, and much of the rest of the world, spellbound. Long before any evidence had been presented in court, millions of people knew what they wanted the verdict to be. On the one side
were those who believed that the first pro-footballer to rush 2,000 yards in a single American
League season could not possibly have murdered his wife. On the other side, were those who
believed that O. J. was too popular, too rich, and just too "nice" for his own good, and that he
was therefore guilty as charged. Logic had little to do with either decision. Race may well have
had much to do with both decisions.

The simple fact was that Simpson's estranged second wife, Nicole Brown Simpson, and her
friend Ronald Goldman were stabbed to death on June 12, 1994. Their bodies were found in the
courtyard of Nicole Brown's condominium in Brentwood, California. The next day, Simpson left
Chicago and returned to Los Angeles, where he was taken in by the LACP for questioning. On
June 17, the day of the funerals of the victims, Simpson made what appeared to be an attempt
at flight in his white Ford Bronco, driven by a friend named A. C. Cowlings. He was pursued and
taken into custody. On July 22, Simpson pleaded "absolutely 100 percent not guilty" to two
counts of first-degree murder.

The criminal trial opened five months later, on January 24, 1995, before Judge Lance A. Ito and
a jury of eight blacks, one white, one Hispanic, and two jurors of mixed race. Marcia Clark led
for the prosecution, Johnnie Cochran for the defense. It was a sensation. A cast selected from
the cream of Hollywood could not have played it better, and viewing figures for what amounted

O. J. Simpson

The LAPD mugshot of O. J. Simpson.

BK 4013970 061794

LOS ANGELES POLICE - JAIL DIV

to a new television soap opera hit the roof. Simpson must have taken some comfort from the knowledge that the prosecution was not seeking the death penalty if the jury decided otherwise. With exquisite timing, O. J. Simpson's book *I Want to Tell You* was published at the height of the trial.

The soap's most dramatic moment came on May 15 when Simpson was asked to put on the bloodstained Aris Light gloves that had been found at the scene of the murders, and were assumed to be those of the murderer. They did not fit. They were too small. "I don't think he could act the size of his hands," said Cochran. "He would be a great actor if he could act his hands larger."

After over 250 days of argument, more than half the population of America watched as the jury delivered its verdict live on television. Simpson was found not guilty. His life since then has not been a happy one. In 1997 a civil jury found him liable for the wrongful death of Ronald Goldman. Simpson was ordered to pay over $33 million in damages. Friends melted away. His acting career never really recovered, but maybe he had already given his finest performance in court.

(*clockwise from bottom right*) The bloodstained front
path to the home of Nicole Brown Simpson, June 14,
1994. A photo of Nicole Brown taken after her 911 call
reporting domestic violence back in January 1989, and
shown in court during O. J. Simpson's trial. The Ford
Bronco and escort on Highway 405, June 17, 1994.
Prosecutor Christopher Darden (far right) looks impas-
sively on as Simpson shows the extra large Aris gloves
that didn't fit, June 21, 1995.

(*opposite*) Supporters and fans of O. J. Simpson celebrate after watching the end of the trial on television, October 2, 1995. (*above*) The team wins through… Simpson and his leading attorneys F. Lee Bailey (left) and Johnnie Cochran (right) hear the jury's "not guilty" verdict.

Mobsters and Monsters

Over 100 members of the Sicilian Mafia in cages in
court in Catanzaro, Italy, on November 1, 1967.
They were on trial for assorted crimes.

In 1900, the square mile of New York City bounded by East 3rd Street, the Bowery, Catherine Street and the East River was home to some 370,000 people, the great majority of them immigrant Jews from Eastern Europe. Crammed into hellish tenements, entire families labored day and night to raise the exorbitant rent on one or two rooms, and men, women, and children died from malnutrition and endemic disease.

Jewish charities did what they could to support these families, subsidizing their rents and encouraging children to attend school, but the system was against them. There were labor laws to forbid children under 14 from working in factories or sweat shops, but there was no law to prevent even a three-year-old from spending up to 12 hours a day doing piecework at home. The photographer and journalist Jacob Riis described the conditions in which such children lived and worked at the end of the 19th century: 'The poverty… is black and bitter; they crowd as do no other living things to save space, which is rent… They slave and starve to make money…' Later Mary Van Kleeck published a report into Child Labor in New York City Tenements. It was an appalling account of child exploitation: of a family where three sisters earned just 80 cents a day making 1,440 artificial roses; of a household where every member of a family was paid 5 cents for making black violets; of three-year-old girls sewing buttons on smart gloves.

The conditions here and in Little Italy drove some to crime, but the real crime lay in generations of children being deprived a childhood. Meanwhile, their older brothers and sisters toiled all day in Lower East Side sweatshops. When a fire broke out at the Triangle Shirtwaist Company near Washington Square on March 25, 1911, 125 Italian and Jewish girls were killed – caught in the flames, or jumping to their deaths. An investigation into the tragedy revealed that exits had been locked to prevent the girls making unauthorized visits to the washrooms.

Lower East Side

Idle hands in the alley known as "Bandits Roost", off Mulberry Street, New York City in 1887.

It took time for Prohibition to affect every American drinker. Some states had already banned the sale and consumption of liquor long before 1919, and when the Prohibition Bill was given its final ratification in January of that year not all alcohol was banned immediately. Whiskey lasted a little longer than beer. It was not until December that the U.S. Prohibition Commissioner banned alcohol based hair-tonics or medicines, and the much-loathed Volstead Act did not take full effect until January 16, 1920.

Criminals, big time and small time, had thus had plenty of time to prepare for the great day when the production, distribution, and sale of liquor would fall into their hands. Legitimate bars and clubs now had to rely on illegitimate sources of supply. The night convoys of trucks began to roll across the Canadian and Mexican borders, the illicit stills multiplied in woods and canyons ("don't use no green or rotten wood, they'll get you by the smoke"), and the ships chartered by mobsters began to unload their 70 proof cargoes along the east and west seaboards – ships carrying alcohol were banned from American ports in October 1922.

As bootlegging spread, so did steps to stamp it out. The first big bust on New York speakeasies came in September 1920, when 50 saloons were raided. Texas began anti-bootleg air patrols in April 1923. In August that year, 84 bootleggers were arrested in a single raid in Savannah, Georgia. Signs of greater trouble ahead came in December 1923 when Emmanuel Kessler, self-styled "King of the Bootleggers" was sentenced to two years imprisonment after bringing in some 5,000 cases of "Auld Scottie" whiskey and 1,300 cases of champagne. The prosecutor in the case, Major John Holley Clark Jr., claimed that he had been offered $100,000 to sabotage his own case. In December 1925, an international "rum ring" was raided, and hundreds of kegs were destroyed. The following year came the first reports that prohibition was directly responsible

Bootlegging

A revenue agent shows how whisky is smuggled through the streets of the United States at the height of Prohibition.

for an increase in the crime rate – Al Capone, Dutch Schultz, Bugs Moran, Legs Diamond, and hundreds more mobsters would have breathed "Amen" to that.

By 1928 deaths from poisoning by illicit alcohol were beginning to rise at an alarming rate, with 518 victims that year in New York City alone. Some were predicting civil war if the Volstead Act remained in force. In 1929 President Herbert Hoover appointed a commission to study the effects of Prohibition on crime in the United States. The number of killings steadily rose – by agents in raids, by mobsters, by rival bootleggers.

Finally, at 5:32 P.M. on December 5, 1933, Prohibition came to an end, and the bars, that had been illegally full for 14 years, were crowded.

(*above*) A shoe worn by moonshiners and made from cowheels, the tracks from which would deceive revenue agents. (*right*) "Happy days are here again…" Stockpiles of beer at a New York brewery shortly after the repeal of Prohibition, April 3, 1933.

Murder Inc. was established in Brooklyn in the late 1920s. Its founding fathers were Joe Adonis, Martin "Buggsy" Goldstein, and Abe "Kid Twist" Reles (a man whose nickname derived from his proven ability as a strangler). Most of Murder Inc.'s recruits were local boys, from Ocean Hill, Brownsville, and East New York. They were paid a regular salary, plus a fee that ranged from $1,000 to $5,000 for each contract killing. Some customers preferred to pay an annual subscription: Lepke Buchalter paid $12,000 per year for the services of the Brooklyn Boys. Fringe benefits included gifts to the parents of the killers, and the provision of the best lawyers in town when things went wrong.

Contracts came from Mafia bosses all over the States. Calling in a hitman from out of town was seen as a smart move. When a "stoolie" or renegade mob member was murdered in Chicago or Pittsburgh, the police looked for a local culprit while the Murder Inc. hitman had already left town and was heading for home.

Leaders came and went. By the 1930s Lepke Buchalter, Meyer Lansky, and Albert Anastasia had joined Reles on the board. Business was brisk. No project was too big, as they proved when a Murder Inc. killer knocked off the notorious gangster Dutch Schultz. But with such a psychotic board of directors there was always the risk that someone would go too far. That someone was Reles, a moral imbecile who had lost count of the number of people he had killed.

A Murder Inc. employee named Harry Rudolph was framed for murder. Questioned by District Attorney Burton B. Turkus, he named Abe Reles and others as responsible for a whole series of killings. A few days later Mrs. Reles walked into Turkus's office. Abe wished to talk. It was a sensational development.

Murder Inc.

Police taking finger prints in a barber shop at the Park Sheraton Hotel, New York, on October 1, 1957, shortly after the murder of Albert Anastasia.

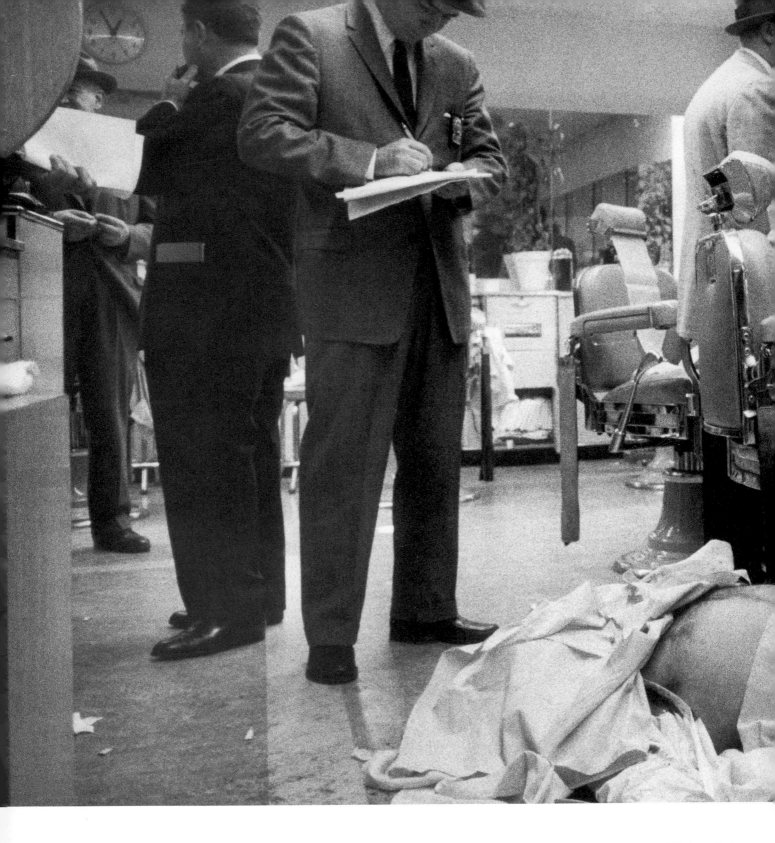

Death of The Lord High Executioner. Albert Anastasia lies on the floor of the barber shop of the Park Sheraton Hotel, New York City, October 25, 1957. After the first volley of shots fired into his body, Anastasia is said to have leapt from the chair and lunged at the reflections of his assassins in the barber's mirror.

Reles had been arrested on average every 78 days between 1932 and 1940, but on almost every occasion had beaten the rap. He believed he could outsmart any lawyer or detective, and was hugely confident when he began his negotiations with Turkus. The deal was that the law was not to

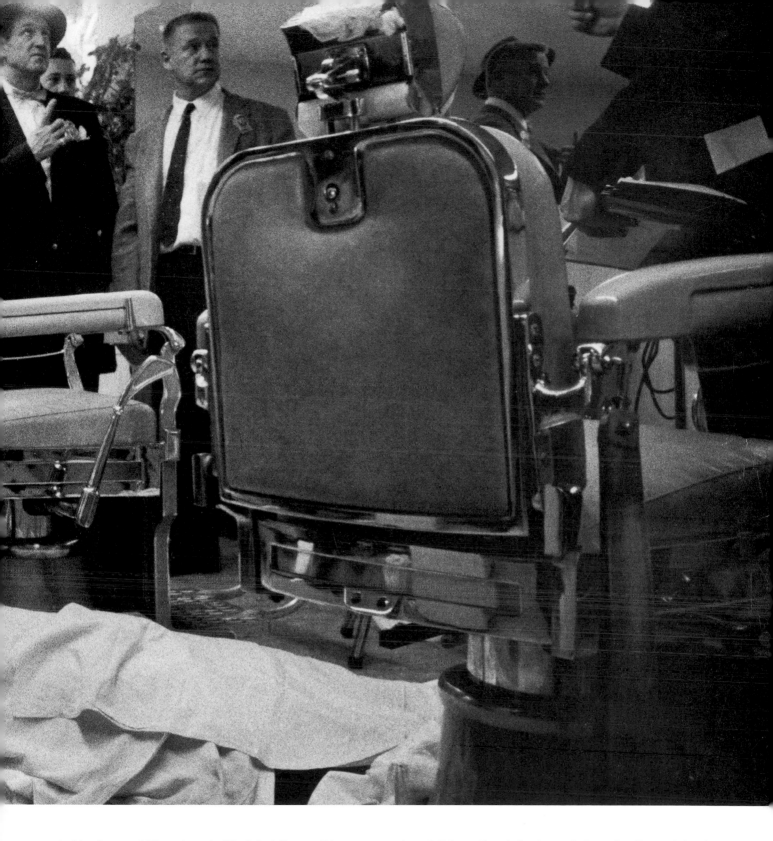

prosecute him for any killings he admitted, but if something new turned up, the law could proceed against him. He talked for two weeks and his prize gift to the authorities was to finger Louis Lepke Buchalter. Both men died violently. Reles, surrounded by half a dozen cops for his own protection, somehow fell from the sixth story window of a Coney Island hotel. Lepke Buchalter was executed in Sing Sing on the night of March 2, 1944. It was the beginning of a swift end for Murder Inc.

In a century that many perceived as the most violent in history, one man of violence achieved a unique fame. 60 years after his death, Alphonse Capone remains the most notorious gangster and mobster of all time. He was a man with great physical strength – capable of clubbing people to death with a single blow – considerable intelligence, and no scruples whatsoever. At the height of his power he controlled gambling houses, race tracks, brothels, speakeasies, nightclubs, distilleries, and breweries, with interests in a number of legitimate enterprises.

He was born in Brooklyn on January 17, 1899. In this tough neighbourhood he joined a couple of "kid gangs" known as the Brooklyn Rippers and the Forty Thieves Juniors, before graduating to work as a bouncer and bartender at Frankie Yale's Harvard Inn. For all its fancy title, it was a rough joint, and it was here that Capone was cut about the face by an angry customer, thus gaining his lifelong nickname "Scarface". Capone always gave as good as he got, however, and in 1919 Yale sent Capone and his family to Chicago, the idea being that they would stay there until things cooled down.

Capone and the Chicago of the Roaring Twenties were made for each other. On Yale's advice, he joined John Torrio's gang, soon taking over as leader when Torrio was wounded in an assassination attempt by a rival gang and decided to retire. By the late Twenties, Capone's income was reckoned to be $100 million a year – on which he paid no income tax. Life was good. There was only one drawback. Although the Mayor of Chicago, "Big Bill" Hale Johnson Jnr. was corrupt, he drew the line at working with Capone, claiming that the mobster was bad for his political image. Capone had to look elsewhere for a family home, and eventually bought a property in Palm Island, Florida.

Al Capone

Alphonse "Scarface" Capone hits the big time and makes the cover of *Time* magazine, March 24, 1930.

TIME

The Weekly Newsmagazine

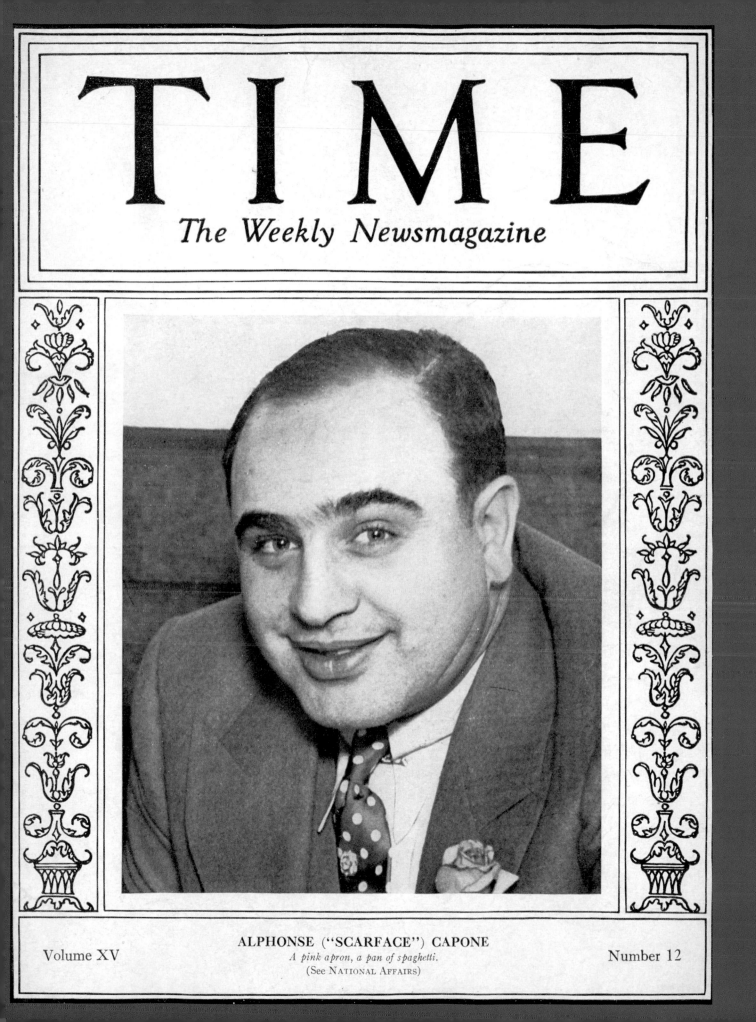

Volume XV

ALPHONSE ("SCARFACE") CAPONE
A pink apron, a pan of spaghetti.
(See NATIONAL AFFAIRS)

Number 12

It was a convenient location for an alibi. On a freezing cold St. Valentine's Day in 1929, the rivalry between Capone and Bugs Moran came to a head. Capone's henchman Jack McGurn led a team of four hit-men to wipe out Moran at the SMC Company Garage at 2122 North Clark. The bait was a fake bootlegging deal that Moran was unlikely to refuse – a delivery of whiskey. McGurn's men arrived in a stolen police car, and Moran, believing a real raid was in progress, slipped away. Six members of his gang, and one innocent bystander, entered the garage and were slaughtered. The finger pointed at Capone. It was a classic Capone-style hit. But Capone had been a thousand miles away, sunning himself in Florida.

Capone was seldom in jail. He was arrested in 1926 for killing three people, but spent only one night behind bars. Three months after the St. Valentine's Day Massacre, he was imprisoned for carrying a gun. Despite being top of the list of Chicago's Most Wanted Criminals in 1930, Capone remained free to walk the blood-splattered streets, but the success of Capone's business enterprises was about to catch up with him. In 1931, he was indicted for income tax evasion. The government charged that he owed $215,000 in back taxes from his gambling profits. Capone pleaded guilty in the belief that he would be able to plea bargain.

Judge James H. Wilkerson refused to cut a deal. Capone changed his plea to "not guilty" and tried to bribe the jury, but Wilkerson switched the jury at the last minute. Capone was found guilty on just five of the 23 counts against him. It was enough. He was sentenced to a total of 10 years in federal prison and one year in the county jail.

In jail, Capone was a model prisoner. He furnished his cell with rugs, a typewriter and a complete set of the

(*clockwise from top left*) Bugs Moran, leader of the North Side Gang in Chicago, 1928. Members of Moran's mob, and one innocent bystander, lie on the floor of the garage at 2122 North Clark, February 14, 1929. The gun said to have been used by Capone on one of the rare occasions when he pulled the trigger. "Machine Gun Jack" McGurn with his wife "the blonde alibi" Louise Rolf on February 15, 1936 – McGurn worked for Capone and led the team of hit-men that wiped out Moran.

Encyclopedia Britannica, and refused to take part in any strikes or prison riots. He served most of his sentence in Alcatraz, much of it in the hospital, for he was diagnosed as suffering from syphilitic dementia.

He was released in November 1939 and returned to his home in Palm Island. The dementia worsened, and Capone was forced to live a quiet life. On January 21, 1947, he suffered an apoplectic stroke unrelated to his syphilis,

contracted pneumonia and died four days later of cardiac arrest. He was initially buried at the centre of his empire, on Chicago's South Side, but a year later his remains were removed to Mount Carmel Cemetery on the West Side.

To many, he is still the greatest mobster of all time.

QUI RIPOSA
GABRIELE CAPONE
NATO DE ... 1920
... O NOV ... 4.1920
QUI RIPOSA
SALVATORE CAPONE
NATO TI ... LIO 16. 1895
MORT ... APRILE 1.192 ...

AL CAPONE
1899 — 1947

REST IN PEACE
CAPONE

(*left to right from far left*) The law enforcer and leader of The Untouchables, Eliot Ness, sits at his desk in the early 1930s. Capone plays cards in a train transporting him to prison, October 1931. Al Capone's tombstone in Mount Carmel Cemetery, June 1948.

By the time he was 14, Arthur Flegenheimer had worked out that he would never get rich through honest toil. Three months later he received his first and only prison sentence, which he served on Blackwell's Island, a brutal institution on New York's East River. On his release, his fellow Bronx gang members gave him his professional name – "Dutch Schultz".

Dutch was a mobster in the roughest mould. He had no sense of compromise, no belief in negotiation. He was a "fight or flight" guy, never seeking some other solution to any problem he faced. He made vast fortunes in bootlegging and an estimated $12 million to $15 million a year from the numbers racket, and plenty more from protection rackets and manipulation of labor unions. He shunned smart clothes. Lucky Luciano called him "one of the cheapest guys I ever knew… a guy with a couple of million bucks and he dressed like a pig".

Dutch was also a vicious man. In his early bootleg days, Dutch kidnapped a rival beer-baron named Joe Rock, hung him by his thumbs on a meat hook, and allegedly then blindfolded Rock's eyes with gauze that had been smeared with the discharge from a gonorrhoea infection. Rock lost his sight. When Dutch learnt that a partner had been creaming money from the take, Dutch whipped out a gun in the presence of his astonished lawyer, stuck it in the partner's mouth and pulled the trigger. Later, he took time to cut out the victim's heart.

He trusted no one, had no friends. In the end, it was a race between the law and other mobsters as to who would get him first. The mobsters won. On October 23, 1935, Charles Workman, a gunman hired by Murder Inc., walked into the Palace Chop House looking for Dutch. He found him in the men's room. The one bullet that hit Dutch ripped through his abdomen, large intestine, gall bladder, and liver. Dutch died 12 hours later. In what was seen as a deliberate snub to this unlovable man, his fellow mobsters sent only four floral tributes to his funeral.

Dutch Schultz

Arthur Simon Flegenheimer, professionally known as Dutch Schultz, awaits the verdict in a tax case against him. This time he got away with it.

His name was originally Usher H. Fellig, and he was born in the Ukraine in 1899. Some 11 years later his family emigrated to New York City, where he changed his first name to Arthur, but it was as plain "Weegee" that he became famous. It took time.

He began his photographic career on leaving school in 1913, later working as a darkroom technician for Acme Newspapers (UPI). He had his first pictures published in 1935. Three years later he shrewdly changed his name to Weegee and adopted both a style and a field of interest that brought him to the attention of picture editors across the United States.

He obtained a police radio and installed it in his car. Using this, he was able to learn exactly where crimes had been recently committed and ensure that he was the first photographer on the scene. Once there, carrying his huge plate camera and with a cigar stuck firmly in his mouth, he not only took pictures of the victims, the neighborhood, and – if he was lucky – the culprit, but habitually rearranged the corpse or added a gun to make his pictures more sensational. To make sure that his talent did not go unnoticed, he also stamped the prints that he sent to newspapers and magazines "Weegee the Famous".

It all worked. In 1941 he had his first one-man exhibition – "Weegee: Murder is My Business" – and four years later came his first book *Naked City*. He moved to Hollywood, appeared as an extra (sometimes playing himself) in black-and-white "mean street" crime movies, and then began to explore the possibilities of portrait photography using distorted images. He made some short films of his own, traveled to the USSR and Europe, gave lectures and even acted as film consultant on Stanley Kubrick's *Dr. Strangelove*. He died in 1968.

Weegee's World

Weegee's crime scene picture of the gangster Dominick Didato, killed for interfering in Lucky Luciano's racketeering, July 1936.

But it will always be as a New York crime photographer that Weegee will be remembered. His late night pictures of run-of-the-mill crimes, of domestic violence, of death on the street, of world-weary cops and dazed assailants, and of those moments when crime seems more silly than terrible, portray the very essence of existence in the poor and sleazy tenements that still made up so much of New York in the days of the World War II. As William McCleery wrote of him: "He will take his camera and ride off in search of new evidence that his city, even in her most drunken and disorderly and pathetic moments, is beautiful".

Weegee forged good relationships with many cops on the beat, and his presence at crime scenes and in police precincts was generally accepted by the NYPD. (*above*) A police line-up of suspects photographed by Weegee in 1939. (*opposite*) Weegee (with camera) in action some time in 1945. It would seem that this is one of his many "staged" crime pictures.

Francesco Castiglia was four years old when his family emigrated from Calabria to the States in 1895. His early criminal training took place in New York's East Harlem, where he changed his name to Frank Costello and, with the coming of Prohibition in 1919, he was ready to join forces with Lucky Luciano in bootlegging and gambling enterprises. As the years passed, Costello gained a reputation as being the guy who could buy-off anyone – police, politicians, even judges. In 1936, when Luciano was sent to Dannemora prison in upstate New York, he chose Costello as the family's acting boss. Costello didn't let him down, increasing profits across the country – from slot machines in New Orleans, gambling in Florida (with Meyer Lansky), and illegal race wires in LA (with Bugsy Siegel).

An intense rivalry developed between Costello and Luciano's other lieutenant, Vito Genovese. For a while this didn't matter, for Genovese fled from the States in 1951 fearing that he was about to be charged with murder. Six years later, however, he was back. Genovese hired Vincente "The Chin" Gigante to get rid of Costello, but Gigante made the mistake of shouting "Frank, this is for you!" just before he pulled the trigger. Costello spun round, ducked, and the shots merely grazed his head. Gigante fled, and later turned himself in to the police.

Costello and Genovese came to terms. Genovese wished to deal with the other family member that he loathed, Albert Anastasia. When Anastasia was gunned down on October 25, 1957, Costello called up his old associates Luciano and Lansky. Together they framed Genovese, Gigante and Carmine Galante so that all three went down on a drugs charge. Genovese died in prison. Costello remained busy, operating from New York's Waldorf Astoria until he died of a heart attack in 1973. When Carmine Galante was released from prison, he paid his respects to the man who had framed him by blowing up the doors to Costello's tomb.

Frank Costello

Frank Costello draws comfort during a Senate hearing on organized gambling, 1950.

Salvatore Luciana was born in Sicily, Italy, in 1896 and arrived in New York 10 years later. It did not take long for him to team up with two other kids, named Meyer Lansky and Bugsy Siegel, and start a two-cent protection racket. The trio prospered and, within a year of the introduction of Prohibition, Charles Luciano (as he was now known) was working as a bootlegger for Frank Costello and Vito Genovese.

After a spell in jail, Luciano joined Joe Masseria's gang, becoming second-in-command in 1925. Four years later open warfare broke out between Masseria and a rival Sicilian gang led by Salvatore Maranzano. Luciano was captured by Maranzano's men who stabbed him with an ice pick, slit his throat, and left him for dead on Staten Island beach. It was his miraculous survival that earned him the name "Lucky" Luciano.

Lucky was ambitious. In April 1931 Joe Masseria was killed in a Coney Island restaurant while Luciano, in true Pontius Pilate style, washed his hands in the bathroom. He now became Maranzano's second-in-command, but not for long. Luciano and Lansky learnt that Maranzano was planning to have three men eliminated – Al Capone, Vito Genovese, and Lucky himself. Four of Lansky's associates raided Maranzano's office and killed him. On their way in they met Vincent "Mad Dog" Coll, the man Maranzano had hired to kill Luciano. Not knowing who he was they simply told Coll that they were government agents. Coll fled.

Luciano had what he wanted. He was top man in New York, but had a greater sense of diplomacy than most Mafia leaders. He divided the city into several territories, each controlled by a different Family, under the control of La Commissione, a governing body presided over by Luciano. The system was effective, but in 1936 Luciano was found guilty, on perjured evidence, of

Lucky Luciano

Lazy-eyed and full of menace – a portrait of
Lucky Luciano from 1935.

procuring for immoral purposes and was sentenced to between 30 and 50 years in jail.

Luciano spent World War II in prison, arranging Mafia assistance for the U.S. government and U.S. forces in Italy, clearing the way for the invasion of Sicily, and easing the progress of U.S. troops as they fought their way through Italy. At the same time, he used his Mafia connections to remove Communist influence in the Italian resistance and local government.

In return, the patriot mobster was paroled immediately after the war, on condition that he returned to Italy. Luciano agreed, stopping off in Cuba for the famous Havana Conference where he and Lansky arranged the execution of their childhood playmate, Bugsy Siegel. There were numerous threats on Lucky's life subsequently, but when he died it was from a heart attack at Naples International Airport. His body was returned to the United States and buried in St. John's Cemetery, Queens.

(*top*) Luciano (third from right) enjoys a stroll through Lercara, Sicily, in 1949. (*below*) In busier days, Luciano (hands to face) is booked at a New York City courtroom desk early in 1935. (*opposite*) The luck runs out – the body of Charles "Lucy" Luciano lies on the ground at Naples Airport, January 26, 1962.

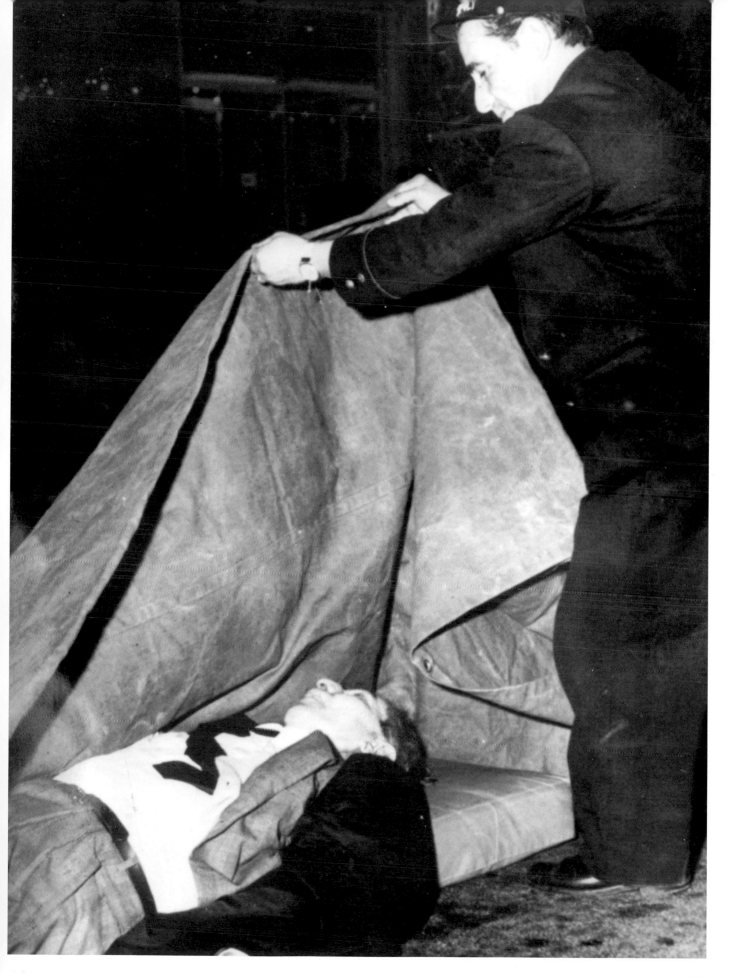

Benjamin Siegelbaum disliked his nickname intensely. It was wiser to call him "Ben", better still to call him "Mr Siegel". The first half of his short life was the routine mobster progression from rags to racketeering. He was born in 1905 in Hell's Kitchen, Brooklyn, where he ran protection rackets with a weak-willed friend named Moey Sedway, before meeting the man who was to be a major influence in his life and the instigator of his death – Meyer Lansky. Bugsy's first murder was a revenge killing. Lucky Luciano, an associate of Lansky, was sent down on a drugs charge. Bugsy and Lansky decided to execute the 19-year-old witness responsible for the conviction. The boy's body was never found. A local woman who claimed she had information on the killing was savagely beaten. Bugsy met the woman by chance eight years later, raped her and threatened her with worse if she went to the police.

Bugsy would have been just another vicious racketeer making money from bootlegging and gambling dens. What gave him a place in history began with his move to California in 1937. He bought a 35-room mansion in Hollywood, took control of the unions that supplied labor to the film industry, and slid into glamorous society. His good looks, considerable charm, and ruthless business methods brought him the power to shut down every studio in town. At the same time he collected money from the stars to prevent him doing just that.

After World War II Bugsy hit on the idea of building a top hotel and casino in the sandy wastes of the Nevada Desert at a little place called Las Vegas. At first the project proved a nightmare, but by May 1947 both hotel and casino were up and running and Bugsy had cleared his debts. He had less than a month to enjoy his success. His old partner Meyer Lansky suspected that Bugsy was hiding some of the profits they were jointly making. On June 20, while he was relaxing in his Beverly Hills home, Bugsy was shot four times in the chest. He died almost instantly.

Bugsy Siegel

The man who made Las Vegas the gambling Mecca of the United States – Bugsy Siegel lights up at the height of his power, 1940.

When United Airlines Flight 629 exploded in mid-air minutes after leaving Stapleton Airport, Denver, Colorado on the evening of November 1, 1955 there were no survivors. Among the dead was Mrs. Daisie King, a passenger flying to Seattle en route to visit her daughter in Alaska. Her son, Jack Graham, had accompanied her to the airport and had been anxious to get her aboard the plane.

There was reason for his concern. Inside his mother's luggage, wrapped up to look like a Christmas present, was a bomb constructed from 25 sticks of commercial dynamite, two blaster caps, a small battery, and – crucially – a timer set to last only 90 minutes. Graham knew this, for he had made the bomb and packed it in his mother's suitcase. When the plane took off, Graham went to the airport cafeteria where he took a cup of coffee and ate a doughnut. Soon news came through of the disaster. Forty-four people had been killed.

The tragedy was investigated by the FBI, who soon found discrepancies in Graham's account of his movements during the last couple of days before the disaster. They also learnt that Graham had a simmering hatred towards his mother, whom he believed had ill-treated him during his early life. Graham's wife told them about the package that Graham had placed in his mother's luggage. He was arrested on November 14 and charged with 44 counts of murder. There was no doubt of his guilt and Graham was sentenced to death. He made no attempt to appeal against the sentence.

In prison, Graham tried to hang himself in his cell, but was cut down, rushed to the prison hospital and made a full recovery. His execution was set for January 12, 1957. At 7:45 P.M. he walked quietly to the gas chamber where he was strapped into a metal chair. Almost his last words were: "Everybody pays their way and takes their chances. That's just the way it goes."

Jack Graham

Jack Graham, surrounded by FBI detectives after killing his mother and 43 other people.

In 1951 a prison report on 17-year-old Charles Manson described him as "…a slick institutionalized youth… dangerous… should not be trusted across the street…" Seven years and several crimes later, Manson was said to be "… a very shaky probationer and it seems just a matter of time before he gets into further trouble." Up to this point, however, Manson's crimes had been of a comparatively petty nature – minor theft, driving a stolen car across state lines, assault, and passing stolen cheques. Although he had spent almost half his life in prison, Manson was still a long way from deserving the title he was later given of "the symbol of ultimate evil".

Big trouble came in the 1960s. While serving a 10-year sentence on McNeil Island, Washington State, Manson raped another inmate at razor point. This was violence at a new level. Against his own wishes, Manson was released in March 1967 and moved to the Haight-Ashbury area of San Francisco where he began recruiting what others referred to as his "Family". With a group of some 30 hard-core followers, Manson left the city to take over a disused ranch in the San Fernando Valley. Here he cultivated pseudo-religious status. He became interested in some of the weirder movements of the age – the Church of the Final Judgement, the Church of Satan, and the Circe Order of Dog Blood. He also encouraged his Family to believe that he was the reincarnation of Christ.

Then in August 1969, came the two nights when the Family indulged in an horrendous orgy of killing. At midnight on August 8, under orders from Manson, but without their leader's presence, a group of his followers drove out to film director Roman Polanski's Beverly Hills home. Polanski was away, filming in London. It made no difference. The Family shot a friend of the gardener, then entered the house and rounded up the four occupants – Jay Sebring, Wojciech

Charles Manson

The eyes and "x" scar on the forehead of Charles Manson, the cult-leader who claimed that he was "the mad dog killer fiend leper" that reflected the society he lived in.

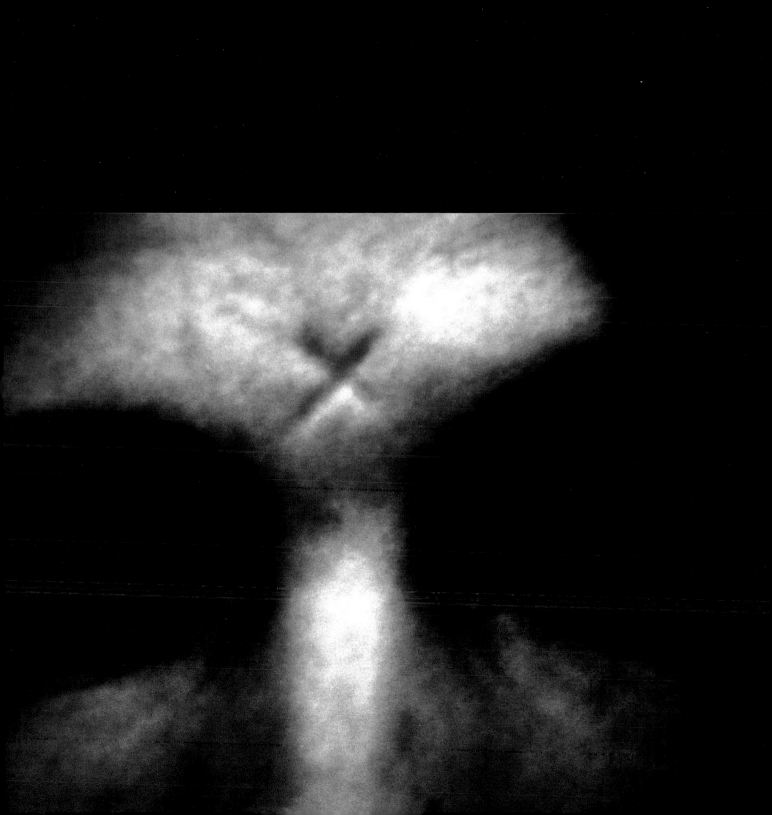

Frykowski, Abigail Folger, and the film star Sharon Tate. Sebring was shot, Frykowski was bludgeoned to death, Folger was repeatedly stabbed. Sharon Tate, Polanski's wife, who was eight months pregnant, begged for the life of her unborn child. One of the killers, Susan Atkins, replied: "Look, bitch, I don't care if you are having a baby. You are going to die and I don't feel a thing about it." Atkins then stabbed her to death.

The following night, Manson took three members of the Family, two of whom had been involved in the previous killings, to the home of Leno and Rosemary LaBianca. Manson reportedly told his followers he was going "to show them how to do it", how to kill without indulging such mayhem. No other motive for this crime has been discovered.

At Manson's trial it was suggested that he believed a global race war was imminent, which "the Blacks" would win. The Family would be able to sit out this war in peace in a secret underground world reached via a hole in the Californian desert, to emerge as leaders when the war was over. The Tate and LaBianca killings had taken place because "the Blacks" were unable or unwilling to precipitate the war, and had therefore to be shown how to do it.

On March 29, 1971, Manson was sentenced to death. This

(*above*) The front yard of the Barker Ranch, Death Valley, California where Manson and his Family lived through much of 1968 and 1969. It was owned by the grandmother of Catherine Gillies, a Family member. Manson sent Gillies to murder her grandmother, so that she could inherit the ranch, but the plot was foiled by a flat tire. (*right*) The nearby Spahn's Movie Ranch, where the family lived before moving to Barker Ranch.

(*clockwise from top left*) The pregnant film star Sharon Tate, wife of the director Roman Polanski, holds up baby clothes in the back of a London taxi on August 6, 1969, three days before she was murdered. Susan Atkins, one of the killers of Sharon Tate. Roman Polanski sits on the bloodstained porch of his Californian home a few days after the murder of his wife, Sharon Tate. Two members of the Family in the early 1970s.

was later commuted to life in prison after California's Supreme Court invalidated all death sentences imposed in the state prior to 1972. Manson remains in prison today. All his applications for parole have been denied, most famously that of 1986 when he appeared before the board with a swastika embossed on his forehead. It is unlikely that he will ever be released. It is said that he gets over 60,000 pieces of mail a year.

The Family itself survives, and has committed other murders since Manson's incarceration. In September 1975, Lynette Alice "Squeaky" Fromme attempted to assassinate President Gerald Ford in Sacramento, but she had failed to ensure that her gun was loaded. She claimed that the reason for her attempt was that Manson would be called to appear as a witness at her trial and would thereby have a platform from which to reaffirm his apocalyptic vision.

The hole in the desert and the underground world to which it led have not yet been found.

In the late 1950s Jommie Jones established the People's Temple in Indianapolis, later moving to San Francisco. The Temple did not prosper. There were scandals, and by the early 1970s the movement was on the point of collapse. Jones decided to leave the United States and establish a utopian community in Guyana. It was named Jonestown. There were problems from the beginning – lack of adequate food, a brutal work regime, fevers, and outbreaks of severe diarrhea. Discipline was rigorously enforced by armed guards. Offenders were incarcerated in boxes or had electric shocks administered to their genitalia. Would-be deserters were incapacitated by drugs. It was said by survivors that there were harsh beatings. Parents had to surrender guardianship of their children to Jones, who was addressed as "Dad" or "Father" by everyone.

In November 1978 the community was visited by Congressman Leo Ryan and a team of "Concerned Relatives of People's Temple Members", aiming to investigate alleged violations of human rights. Jones did all he could to disrupt the visit, and to give the false impression that all was well in Jonestown. He failed. Many members of the community begged Ryan to take them with him when it was time to leave. Fanatic followers of Jones attacked the plane as it prepared for take-off, killing Ryan, three journalists, a cameraman, and three defectors.

Knowing what would follow, Jones decided to bring the dream-turned-nightmare to an end with a mass suicide. On November 18 a mixture of grape Flavor Aid laced with Valium and cyanide was dispensed to his followers in paper cups. Babies and children were the first to die. The deadly cocktail was squirted down their throats with syringes. Then came the elderly, and finally the adults. Many parents took the poison immediately after watching their children die. A few tried to flee. Most were shot by Jones's guards athough a few managed to escape. Jones died from a gunshot in the head. It is not known if it was self-administered. All in all, 913 of the 1,110 members died, including 276 children. Jonestown itself was destroyed by fire in the mid-1980s.

Jonestown

Bodies of men, women and children cover the ground at Jonestown following the largest mass suicide in modern history, November 18, 1978.

He was known as the "Teflon Don" because so few charges against him could ever be made to stick. To the New York tabloids he was "The Dapper Don", famous for his $1,800 tailor-made suits, his slicked-back silver hair, and his grandiose air. He was a man of whom there were conflicting opinions. To his fellow mobsters he was a great man who gave hand-outs and organized picnics in his Queens neighborhood. "If there were more people like John Gotti on this earth," said his deputy Frank Locascio, "we would have a better country." To his law enforcement enemies he was a Mark 1 villain. "John Gotti is a stone-cold killer… a vicious and ruthless boss," said J. Bruce Mouw, the FBI agent who helped to convict him.

Gotti was born into a blue-collar Bronx family in 1940. He dropped out of grade school and was soon in trouble with the police. In 1966 he moved to Queens and joined the powerful Family run by Carlo Gambino. He graduated, Mafia style, in 1973 when he killed James McBratley, a member of an Irish-American gang said to have kidnapped and killed Gambino's nephew. Gambino supplied a smart lawyer. Gotti was convicted of manslaughter only, and served just two years.

Gambino died and the Family was taken over by his cousin Paul Castellano. On December 16, 1985, Gotti made his move. As Castellano drove up to the Sparks Steak House in Manhattan Castellano's automobile was pumped with bullets from the guns of Gotti and disaffected members of the Gambino family. Gotti became head of the Family.

In 1992 came big trouble. Sammy "the Bull" Gravano made a deal with the government. He gave evidence against Gotti, who was convicted of five murders and sentenced to life without parole. For a while he continued to run the gang from prison, but was too weak physically and politically to do so. Still in prison, he died of cancer in 2001.

John Gotti

John Gotti, "The Dapper Don", is pursued by members of the New York City media as he arrives at the courthouse for his trial in 1992.

On October 16, 1991, the Rev Shannon McMullen was standing in line at Luby's Cafeteria in Killeen, Texas. He was trying to decide "what meats to get". Seconds later a Ford Ranger pickup truck smashed through Luby's window. The driver got out, brandished a Glock 17 and a Ruger P89, and shouted: "This is what Bell County has done to me!" He opened fire.

Barbara Nite and Kitty Davis were knocked from their seats by the truck. As Kitty Davis tapped her hand on her friend's leg, in a attempt to reassure her, a bullet shattered her thumb and Barbara Nite's ankle. McMullen was hit in the leg and took cover under a bench while the worst mass shooting in American history to that date took place all around him. He saw the gunman march up to a woman who was cowering against the far wall. The killer extended his arm, took careful aim, shot the woman in the head, and then turned slowly back to the dining area.

The gunman was George Hennard, an unemployed Belton man. He had only once been in trouble with the police, when he had been arrested in 1981 for possession of marijuana, but he was known to have a volatile temper. The previous day – his 35th birthday – he had been heard screaming with rage at TV coverage of the appointment of Clarence Thomas to the Supreme Court. "You bastards opened the door for all the women!" Hennard yelled.

The shooting and pandemonium continued. One customer threw himself through a plate glass window, which provided an escape route for others. Hennard deliberately spared a four-year-old girl and her mother. The end came quickly when the police arrived. In the ensuing gun battle Hennard was wounded several times. He dragged himself into the hallway, and then killed himself with a shot to the head. In all, Hennard killed 23 people that day, and wounded 20 others.

George Hennard

In the aftermath of the massacre wreaths and flowers decorate the front of Luby's Cafeteria, October 1991.

The Branch Davidian Seventh-Day Adventists were formed in 1959. By 1990 they were led by David Koresh, and their headquarters was a compound at Waco, Texas. At 9:30 A.M. on February 28, 1993 agents of the Bureau of Alcohol, Tobacco and Firearms attempted to serve arrest and search warrants on Koresh and the compound. There was a gun battle. Four ATF agents were killed and 16 wounded. The number of Davidian casualties is not known. The Waco siege began.

It lasted 51 days. The ATF agents were joined by the FBI, Texas Rangers and police, with the FBI leading the operation. From time to time, children and other Davidians were released by Koresh, or managed to break-out, but the authorities became impatient and uneasy. The Davidians were believed to have sufficient food and supplies to last them a year or more. There was talk of cutting off supplies of water and electricity to the compound, but pressure increased to use more direct action to end the stand-off. The besiegers brought up flammable tear-gas canisters and Bradley armored vehicles.

On Sunday, April 18 the FBI warned the Davidians that a move would be made against the compound and ordered them to vacate the compound's tower. The Davidians refused, presenting children at the windows and holding up a sign saying "Flames Await". Early the following morning the assault began with a tear-gas attack that lasted three hours. The end came when flames appeared in the compound, although there is still bitter controversy as to which side started the fire. The White House insisted that those inside the compound were responsible. Others claimed that news footage of burning canisters being fired into the compound by the besiegers mysteriously disappeared after only one showing on TV. A total of 86 people were killed, including 17 children and Koresh himself. There were only nine survivors.

Waco and Aftermath

Flames engulf the observation tower at the Waco Compound, April 19, 1993. There is still controversy as to who started the fire – the besiegers or the besieged.

One of the visitors to Waco while the siege was in progress was a young ex-soldier and hero of the first Gulf War named Timothy McVeigh. Already hostile towards government agencies, McVeigh's anger at what he saw was to have terrifying consequences. On the second anniversary of the ending of the siege and the killing of the Davidians, McVeigh drove a truck up to the Alfred P. Murrah Federal Building in Oklahoma City, just as staff were arriving for work. The truck was loaded with a 5,000 lb. mixture of agricultural fertilizer and a highly volatile motor-racing fuel. McVeigh got out of the truck and a few moments later ignited a time fuse. Hundreds were injured and 168 men, women, and children were killed.

In June 1997 he was convicted of the killing of eight federal employees, and was ultimately executed by lethal injection four years later. He was 33 years old.

(*above*) The north side of the Albert P. Murrah Federal Building, Oklahoma City, April 19, 1995. At the time, it was the worst terror attack in history on American soil. (*opposite*) Timothy McVeigh, in orange prison uniform, arrives at the Oklahoma courthouse two years later. Following his conviction and death sentence, McVeigh initially appealed. In March 1999 the Supreme Court turned down his last appeal, though it was not until June 11, 2001 that McVeigh was executed by lethal injection.

Until the late 1990s few people outside the Balkans had heard of Kosovo, a province of Serbia inhabited largely by ethnic Albanians. Throughout history, the Balkans had been a place of unrest, a vast mountainous cockpit in which war after war was fought, and the scene of numerous insurrections and nationalist rebellions. In the turmoil that followed the death of President Josip Tito of Yugoslavia in 1980, the constituent units of the Yugoslav Federation began to break from one another. In April 1991 open warfare broke out between the Bosnian government and local Serbs.

At the time, Slobodan Milosevic was President of the Serbian Republic. He was a man who held the Serbian cause high and who carried deeply-held grudges concerning the way history, and his country's neighbors, had treated Serbia. As with all wars, the longer fighting continued, the more vicious it became, culminating in a series of atrocities, the most infamous of which was the mass slaughter of Albanians in the southern part of Kosovo in 1999. Dozens of men, women, and children were killed. They were probably civilians, although the Serb police insisted that the men and boys were dressed in the uniform of the Kosovo Liberation Army. After death, the bodies had been mutilated. Eyes had been gouged. Heads had been smashed. Some of the victims had been decapitated.

The world was appalled. Milosevic was called upon to identify those responsible and ensure that they were brought to justice. When he failed to do this, he was himself indicted as a war criminal by the United Nations. In June 2001 he was handed over to the Hague Tribunal, but his spirited attacks on the validity of that court and his skilful use of delaying tactics, resulted in his trial not opening until February 2002. The United Nations Chief Prosecutor Carla del Ponte accused Milosevic of being responsible for "the worst crimes to humankind".

Slobodan Milosevic

Former Yugoslav President Slobodan Milosevic is portrayed as a saint on the walls of the Socialist Party Headquarters, Belgrade, March 13, 2006 – two days after his death.

СЛОБО
ДАН

СРПСКИ

With all this tension, Milosevic's health rapidly began to decline. He was ill for weeks at a time, suffering from heart trouble, high blood pressure, and fatigue. Proceedings were further delayed when the trial's presiding judge resigned for undisclosed health reasons. By that time the trial had already produced over 630,000 pages of evidence and statements. It dragged on for a further four years.

In the end, death intervened. On March 11, 2006, a prison guard found Milosevic dead in his cell. Although his defense attorney suggested that he had been poisoned, it seems probable that ultimately his heart failed. He died leaving the future of Kosovo still the subject of intense dispute.

(*above*) Milosevic is led into the courtroom for his first appearance before the UN Crimes Tribunal at The Hague, July 3, 2001. (*opposite*) The "Death Notice" of Milosevic, placed by his daughter in the Montenegrin daily newspaper *Pobjeda*.

ТАТА

Волим те.

Твоја МАРИЈА

7460(п.в.)

On September 2, 1994 11-year-old Robert Sandifer was taken by people he thought were his friends to a bridge on Southside Chicago. Here he was forced to kneel on the concrete under the arch of the bridge and was killed by a single bullet in the back of the head. It was a gangland execution, for "Yummy", as Robert was known to his fellow gang members, had gunned down a 14-year-old girl a few days earlier. The police response, following the girl's murder, had been rapid and intense, and Yummy's crime and his continued existence placed other gang members at risk.

The two murders shocked the city, for they caused light to be thrown on a dark and deadly sub-culture. Most people were aware that drug dealers and other criminals formed role models for youngsters like Yummy. The lifestyle and accoutrements of such men had appeal – limousines, jewelry, sharp clothes, lots of cash, fear, and respect. The flip side of all this was that children of Yummy's age and younger had an appeal to the gang bosses. Children were employed to act as look-outs and to run errands. Yummy had been arrested dozens of times in his short life, but boys of his age were seldom given custodial sentences and, even if they were, it was not long before they were back on the streets.

What rocked the United States was the revelation that the involvement of such children in the underworld was at a deeper and more violent level – and not just as abused victims. Yummy's killers were themselves children – 16-year-old Derrick Hardaway and his 14-year-old brother Cragg. Both were members of the same gang as Yummy. Both had entered the world of the gang before they were ten. For killing Yummy, both were convicted of murder. Derrick was sentenced to 45 years in prison, Cragg to 60 years.

Robert Yummy Sandifer

Mourners lean over the body of Robert Sandifer, killed by members of his own gang, the Black Disciples, September 7, 1994.

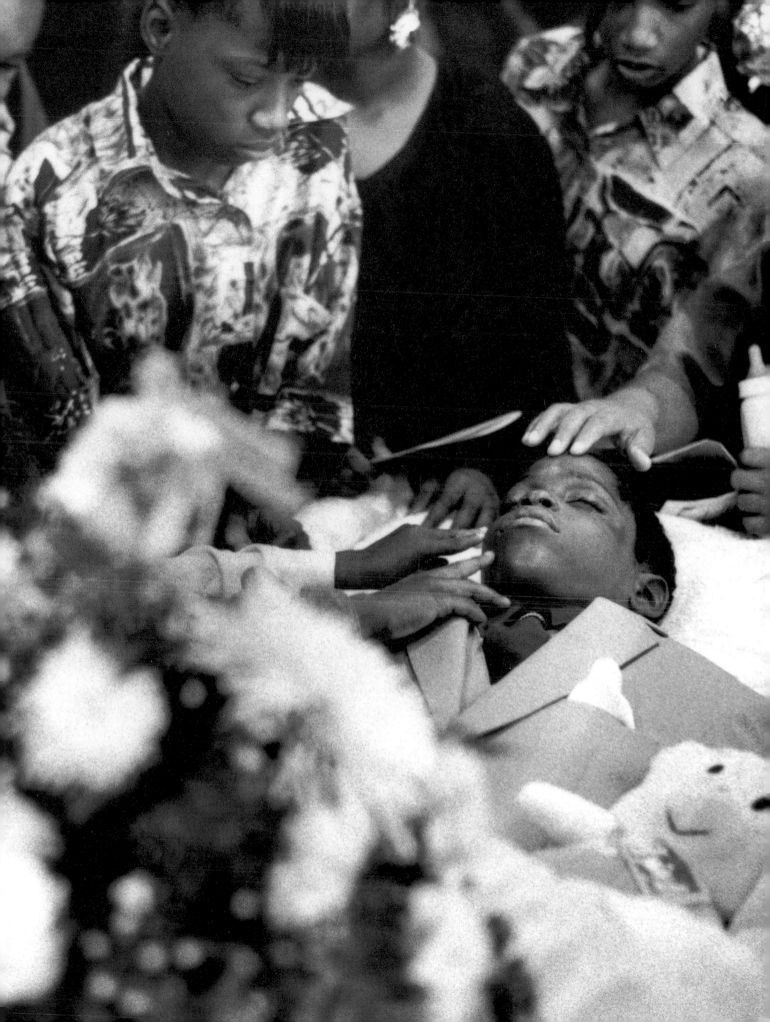

In 1952, at the age of 10, Ted Kaczynski was known to be a bright boy with an IQ of 170. Precociously gifted as a mathematician, he entered Harvard six years later, and in 1967 was hired as an assistant professor at Berkeley. Two years later he resigned without notice or explanation. The "shutdown" side of Kaczynski had taken over.

He was always withdrawn as a child and his mother attributed his behavior to Ted's immediate post-natal separation from her while he was treated for hives. Psychiatrists later postulated that this infection could have caused schizophrenia. Whatever the causes, Kaczynski sought an increasingly remote existence, and in the 1970s went to live in a cabin in Montana.

He sent his first mail-bomb in May 1978, targeting an academic, but the bomb was poorly constructed and did little damage. The next targets were airline officials and a commercial airplane. Again, little harm was done but the FBI became concerned. They christened the perpetrator "The Junkyard Bomber", but Kaczynski was to become notorious as "The Unabomber" (from "university" and "airline" bomber), for Kaczynski's bombs were becoming frighteningly sophisticated. In 1985 he seriously injured a Berkeley graduate student and killed a California computer store owner with nail-and-splinter packed bombs.

For a while there was a lull. In 1993–94 Kaczynski sent one bomb to a computer professor at Yale, another to a geneticist, and a third which killed an advertising executive. He was now operating as the "Freedom Club", whose aim was to prevent computers taking over the world. When the *New York Times* and *Washington Post* published the Unabomber's 35,000-word paper called *Industrial Society and its Future*, Kaczynski's brother recognized the writing style and told the FBI. On April 3, 1996, Kaczynski was arrested at his cabin. After receiving a life sentence, he made an unsuccessful attempt to hang himself. He is still in prison and still writing.

Unabomber

A police photo of Theodore Kaczynski in April 1996, taken in the Lewis and Clark Jail in Helena, Montana, shortly after his arrest on suspicion of being the Unabomber.

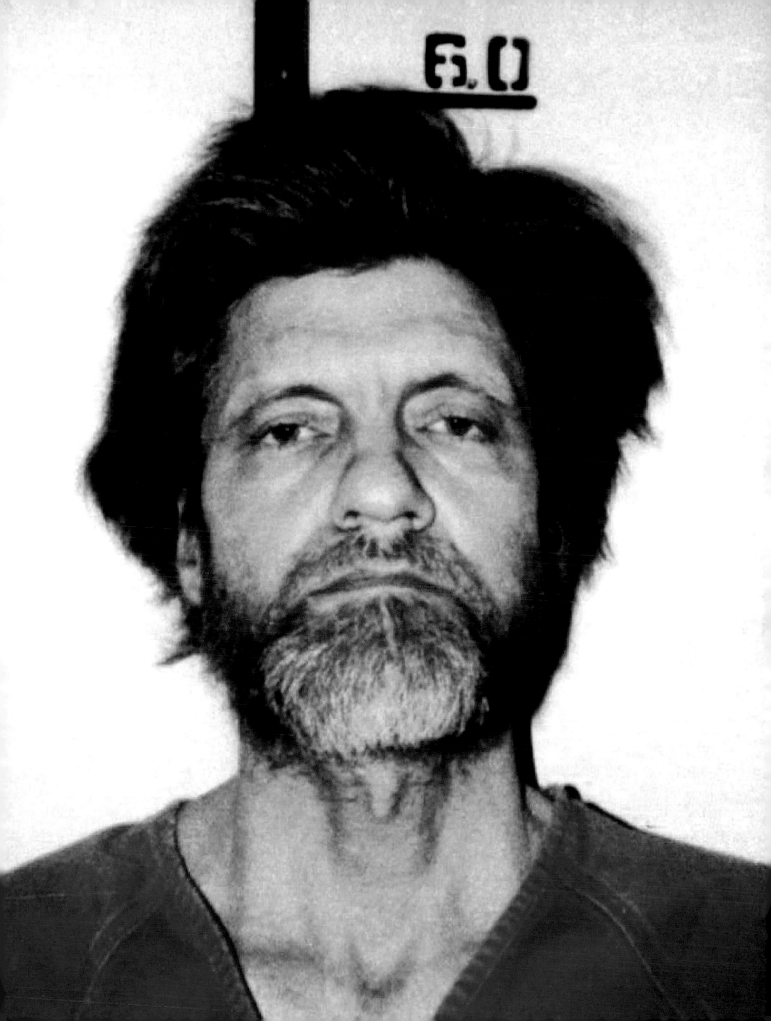

The events of 9/11 marked a new stage in the relationship between the camera and history. Never before had a major historical event received live coverage on this scale. Long before it was clear what was happening, hundreds of millions of onlookers, throughout the planet, were watching it happen. And the images that the world saw on that day were immediate, unedited and uncensored, many of them so horrifying that they have seldom been seen since.

At 8:19 A.M. Eastern District Time, Flight Attendant Betty Ong informed American Airlines that a hijack was in progress on Flight 11 from Boston to Los Angeles. Less than half an hour later, the plane crashed at a speed of 490 mph (788 kph) into the north side of the North Tower of the World Trade Center, New York City. For just 16 minutes it seemed like a terrible accident, but then AA Flight 175 hit the south side of the South Tower, and it became clear that the worst crime ever committed in the United States was taking place. Two more planes had already been reported as having been hijacked – AA Flight 77 (Washington D.C. to Los Angeles) and United Airlines Flight 93 (Newark to San Francisco).

By this time TV and radio networks had live coverage operating. Millions saw the second crash live on TV. Global satellite links were beaming reports and pictures around the world, and on the Internet debate on 9/11 had begun. At 9:36 A.M. AA Flight 77 hit the western wing of the Pentagon, setting fire to the building. All 64 people on board and 125 Pentagon staff were killed. At 9:59 A.M. the South Tower of the WTC collapsed, sending clouds of pulverized concrete and gypsum through the surrounding streets. When the wind eventually blew the dust away, the South Tower was gone.

At 10:00 A.M., knowing something of the fate of the other three hijacked planes, passengers on board Flight 93 began an heroic struggle to wrestle control of the plane from the terrorists. The

9/11

A gallery of those terrorists held responsible for the hijacking of the four flights on September 11, 2001.

Waleed M. Alsheri

Mohammed Atta

Wail M. Alshehri

Abdulaziz Alomari

Satam M.A. al-Suqami

Ahmed Alnami

Ahmed Ibrahim A. al Haznawi

Ziad Samir al-Jarrah

Saeed Alghamdi

Khalid Almihdar

Majed Moqed

Nawaf Alhazmi

Salem Alhazmi

Hani Hanjour

Marwan Alshehhi

Ahmed Alghamdi

Mohand Alshehri

Hamza Alghamdi

**Fayez Rashid
Ahmed Hassan
al-Qadi Banihammad**

hijackers retaliated by deliberately crashing the plane into a field southeast of Pittsburgh.

By 10:30 A.M. the North Tower of the WTC had collapsed and the worst of the damage had been done, although it was not until 5:20 P.M. that the 47-storey 7 World Trade Center building (a third, smaller tower) collapsed. But by now much of the world was now in a state of profound shock. As yet no one knew the extent of the carnage, just how many innocent people – passengers, flight crew, office workers, rescue teams, passers-by – had been killed. Nor did they know the identities of most of the victims. Relatives of those who worked at the Pentagon had a little more time to hope desperately for a miracle and fear that they were intimately involved in the tragedy.

The crimes themselves were appalling. One eye-witness of the moments when both Flight 11 and Flight 175 hit the WTC described how the first impact was followed by a deafening silence, then a flood of radio calls asking for

information. He was a stonemason, working on outer facing of the 60th storey of the old Pan Am building. "We observe what appeared to be an observer plane coming in for a 'look see'. But suddenly it ploughs into the other tower... explosion... fire ball... that's deliberate... all of a sudden it becomes apparent that we are a potential target... everyone starts yelling 'Get down! Get down!'... Huge hanging rigs and crews drop down the sides of the building in record time..."

It was not until 4:00 P.M. that the name Osama bin Laden was officially mentioned in connection with the crimes. Earlier President Bush had broadcast to the world saying:

(top) At 9:36 A.M. Flight 77 crashed into the west side of the Pentagon. (opposite) With smoke erupting from its upper floors, the second of the Twin Towers at the World Trade Center starts to collapse, showering glass, concrete, plaster and debris over the streets of downtown New York.

"Freedom itself was attacked this morning by a faceless coward, and freedom will be defended. The United States will hunt down and punish those responsible for these cowardly acts." The hijackers themselves were, of course, already dead, but it was clear that a crime on this scale needed planning, resources and funding way beyond the capabilities of a handful of terrorists.

That night, after addressing the nation on TV, President Bush wrote in his diary: "The Pearl Harbor of the 21st century took place today. We think it's Osama bin Laden..."

(*above*) Rescue workers stand amidst the wreckage of the World Trade Center two days after the terrorist outrage. Inside the ruins are the bodies of many of their colleagues. (*opposite*) One of the many New Yorkers who were caught in the dust storm that followed the collapse of the Twin Towers takes refuge in another office building.

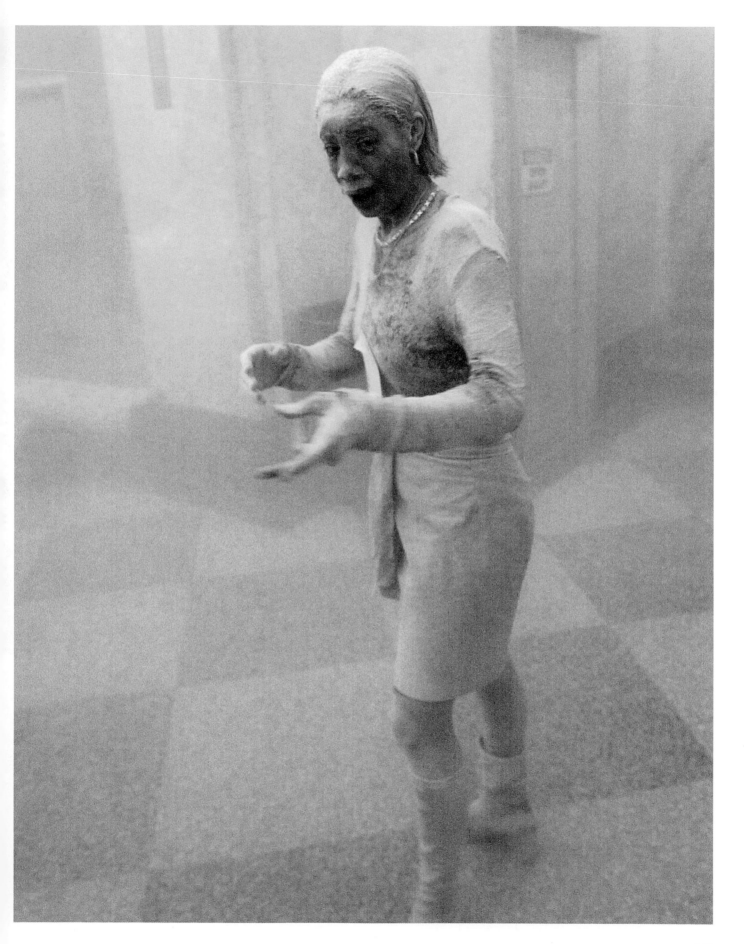

The Columbine High School Massacre of 1999 was a not unique event. Throughout the 1990s there had been at least 20 incidents of armed attacks on schools by students, the great majority of them in the United States. What made Columbine different was that the killers were neither deranged strangers nor terrorists. For two years Eric Harris, one of the two killers, had been posting death-threats against students and teachers at Columbine on his website. He and Dylan Klebold had been rehearsing the massacre. They had kept a journal outlining plans for a major bomb attack, to be followed by the hijacking of a plane at Denver International Airport. This was not to be used to escape, but was to be flown into a major building in New York City.

Harris and Klebold arrived at Columbine at 11:15 A.M. on Tuesday April 20, 1999. They placed two bombs in the school cafeteria, and as they left Harris told Brooks Brown, a student against whom he had posted death threats on his website, to "get out of here". In the car park, Harris and Klebold armed themselves with two sawn-off shotguns, a semi-automatic rifle, and a semi-automatic pistol. They climbed to the highest point on the campus, and began shooting at 11:19 A.M., killing three students and seriously injuring nine others. Klebold then descended the stairs leading to the cafeteria, shooting indiscriminately as he went, before he and Harris headed off toward the Library.

Inside the Library were 55 students, three library staff, and one teacher. Harris ordered them all to stand up. Kelbold shot one of the students. He and Harris sat down and reloaded their weapons. The cycle of taunting, shooting, killing, and reloading continued for some 13 minutes, until Harris and Klebold had had enough.

Columbine and Beslan

A still from one of the five home-made videos shows Eric Harris (*left*) and Dylan Klebold at target practice six weeks before the Columbine High School massacre.

(*clockwise from top left*) A still from the school cafeteria CCTV as Kelbold and Harris begin their attack on fellow students, April 20, 1999. Traumatized students watch as the last of the survivors are evacuated from the school building. A 1998 Columbine High School Yearbook photo of Dylan Klebold. Eric Harris's photo from the 1999 Yearbook.

There were to be only two more deaths, those of Harris and Klebold themselves. For 20 minutes they wandered through the school, hurling bombs and shooting aimlessly into classrooms before returning to the Library. Here, 50 minutes after their arrival at school, they committed suicide, in each case with a single shot to the head. Another three hours were to pass before all the wounded survivors were able to get out of the building.

The appalling events at Beslan's Middle School Number One in Russia in the first week of September 2004 were on a totally different scale.

As the new term began, a group of masked and armed men and women approached from the railway tracks that ran behind the school. They entered the playground, rounded up over 1,000 children and adults and herded them at gunpoint to the Sports Hall, a building 10 metres (32 feet) wide and 25 metres (82 feet) long. Here they confiscated cameras and mobile phones, rigged up a series of bombs and booby-traps, and announced that they were Chechen militants.

It was not long before the killing began. As police rushed into the playground to help the few parents and children who had made a desperate escape bid, the terrorists fired from the windows of the Hall. Some witnesses later reported that they then shot several male teachers inside the school. Russian security forces surrounded the building and, for a while, there was a stand-off. At no time did the terrorists seek to negotiate, though President Putin uncharacteristically announced on Russian TV that this was a definite option. The terrorists then passed their demands to the police – they wanted the release of 24 Chechen separatists who had been arrested in June – but followed this up by taking 20 of their male hostages to the second floor of the Hall and executing them.

The heat was intense. The terrorists turned off the water supply, and both children and hostages had to drink their own sweat and urine. When the children cried, their captors frightened them into silence by firing guns in the air. In fear, filth, and agony, the hostages spent a second night in the Hall. On the morning of Day 3, the mood changed, and at 1:05 P.M. violence erupted.

The terrorists gave Russian paramedics permission to collect the corpses that were putrefying in the sun outside the building. As the paramedics did so, two explosions took place in the Hall. Troops ran forward, firing at the windows. Shooting broke out inside the building. Not until the smoke cleared and the surviving terrorists had retreated, was it possible to begin to assess the extent of the carnage. In all 330 adults and children had died.

One of the 330 victims of the massacre at Beslan Middle School Number One, killed when Chechen Separatists seized and held the school for three days in September 2004.

Serial Killers

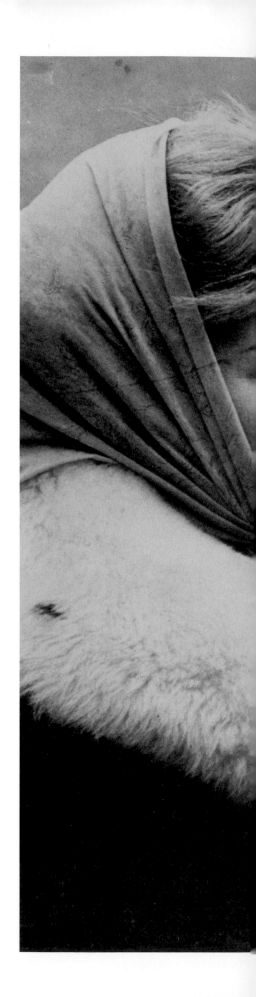

Mrs Ann Downey looks out over the Saddleworth moors,
England on October 18, 1965. Police were looking for
the body of her daughter, Lesley, who had been killed
by the Moors Murderers.

In the 1880s, the East End of London was a tough and desperate place in which to live. It was usual for several families to share one small house or tenement, sleeping on bundles of rags, using an outside lavatory if they were lucky, breathing foul and foetid air, and drinking what could well be contaminated water. Most work was casual – laboring or in the docks – and wages were pitifully low. Life was cheap. Violence and death were regular visitors. A few good souls were pioneering social reform, notably William Bramwell Booth of the Salvation Army and Dr. Thomas Barnado with his East End Mission in Stepney, but by and large the East End remained a dark, bleak, and sordid place where it was still possible for any would-be pimp to buy a young girl for £5 and set her out on a mercifully short lifetime of prostitution.

Vicious though it was, even this world was shocked by what took place in a small area of Whitechapel and Aldgate between August 31 and November 9, 1888. Five women were knifed to death and their bodies grotesquely mutilated. The first to die was Mary Ann Nichols, a 43-year-old prostitute who had gone out to work on the streets that night to earn the four pence she needed for a bed in a lodging house. Her body was discovered at 3:40 A.M. in Buck's Row (now Durward Street). Just over a week later, the body of Annie Chapman was found near a doorway in Hanbury Street. Her throat had been slashed, her abdomen cut open, and her uterus removed. It was estimated that she had been murdered at around 5:30 A.M., when it was already light.

The press reported the murders in elaborate detail. Fear spread throughout London. The police were much criticised and jeered at for their inefficiency. After the second murder a letter was delivered to the Central News Agency, written in red ink and allegedly sent by the killer known

Jack the Ripper

Mortuary sketch of Catherine Eddowes, one of the Ripper's victims, made on September 30, 1888 by Mr. F. W. Foster.

om a sketch taken at the Mortuary by Mr F W Foster

11. A.M. Sunday Septr 30th 1888.

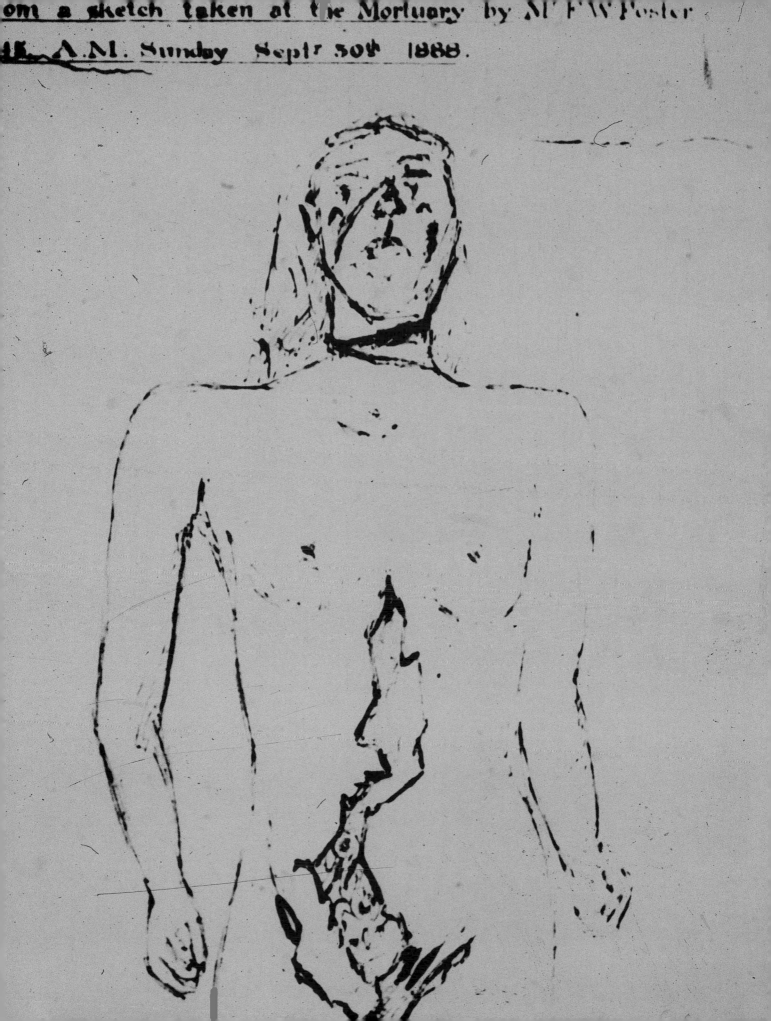

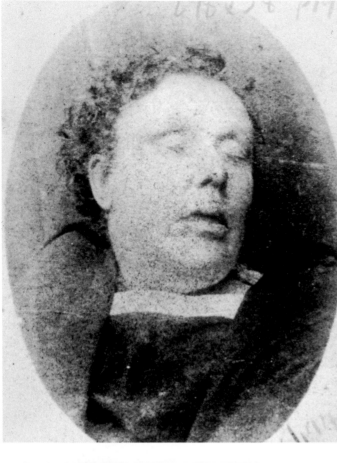

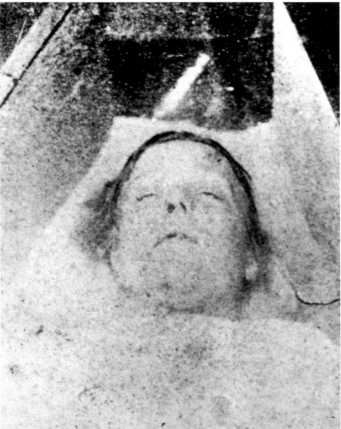

as "Jack the Ripper":

"... I am down on whores and I shan't quit ripping them till I do get buckled. Grand work, the last job was. I gave the lady no time to squeal... I love my work and want to start again. You will soon hear of me and my funny little games...

Good luck,
Yours truly,
JACK THE RIPPER"

Three days later, Elizabeth Stride and Catherine Eddowes were killed on the same night. The steward of a club in Berner Street, Whitechapel found Stride's body at 1:00 A.M., lying in Dutfield's Yard. Her throat had been cut but there

(*clockwise from top left*) Annie Chapman, killed in Hanbury Street on September 8, 1888; Elizabeth Stride, killed in Derner Street, September 30, 1888; front page of London newspaper reporting "Ghastly Murder in the East-End"; Mary Ann Nichols, killed in Buck's Row, August 31, 1888.

GHASTLY
MURDER
IN THE EAST-END.
DREADFUL MUTILATION OF A WOMAN.

Capture : Leather Apron

Another murder of a character even more diabolical than that perpetrated in Buck's Row, on Friday week, was discovered in the same neighbourhood, on Saturday morning. At about six o'clock a woman was found lying in a back yard at the foot of a passage leading to a lodging house in Old Brown's Lane, Spitalfields. The house is occupied by Mrs. Richardson, who lets it out to lodgers, and the door which admits to this passage, at the foot of which lies the yard where the body was found, is always open for the convenience of lodgers. A lodger named Davis was going down to work at the time mentioned and found the woman lying on her back close to the flight of steps leading into the yard. Her throat was cut in a fearful manner. The woman's body had been completely ripped open, and the heart and other organs laying about the place, and portions of the entrails round the victim's neck. An excited crowd gathered in front of Mrs. Richardson's house and also round the mortuary in old Montague Street, whither the body was quickly conveyed. As the body lies in the rough coffin in which it has been placed in the mortuary — the same coffin in which the unfortunate Mrs. Nicholls was first placed — it presents a fearful sight. The body is that of a woman about 45 years of age. The height is exactly five feet. The complexion is fair, with wavy dark brown hair; the eyes are blue, and two of her teeth have been knocked out. The nose is rather large and prominent.

were no other wounds. It is possible that the Ripper's work had been interrupted by the arrival of the steward. Less than three quarters of an hour later, the body of Eddowes was found in a dark corner of Mitre Square. Her wounds were almost identical to those of Annie Chapman.

The Ripper rapidly passed into folk-lore. The number of his victims was exaggerated – there are still those who say that he murdered 18 women in all and that the killings continued until April 1891. There was wild speculation as to the identity of the man with the leather apron and the bloodstained knife. He was said to be a sailor, a doctor, a priest. Modern analysts have accused Lewis Carroll, Francis Thompson, Walter Sickert, James Maybrick (husband and alleged victim

(above left) James Maybrick, a wealthy cotton merchant thought for some time to have been Jack the Ripper – he was poisoned by his wife in 1889. (above right) William Withy Gull, royal physician to Queen Victoria and another major suspect in the Ripper case. (opposite) Buck's Row in 1888, the scene of the murder of Mary Ann Nichols.

of Florence Maybrick), the abortionist and poisoner Dr. T. Neill Cream, and various members of the Royal Family (including Dr. William Gull, physician to Queen Victoria) of being the Ripper, but his identity has never been discovered.

Strangely and unintentionally, the Ripper may have done the East End a service. Shortly after the death of Annie Chapman, on September 8, *The Daily Telegraph* published an editorial on "Dark Annie": "Dark Annie's spirit still walks Whitechapel, unavenged by justice… And yet even this forlorn despised citizeness of London cannot be said to have suffered in vain… She has forced innumerable people who never gave a serious thought before to the subject to realize how it is and where it is that our vast floating population – the waifs and strays of our thoroughfares – live and sleep at night and what sort of accommodation our rich and enlightened capital provides for them. After so many Acts of Parliament passed to improve the dwellings of the poor, and so many millions spent by our Board of Works… 'Dark Annie' will effect in one way what fifty Secretaries of State could never accomplish."

The tale of Bluebeard is believed to have been based on the evil deeds of a 15th-century Breton multiple-murderer named Gilles de Rais. The true story of the man who came to be known as "Bluebeard" begins in 1908. In that year, 39-year-old Henri Landru embarked on the scheme that was to result in the deaths of 10 women, one man, and two dogs.

Landru was a swindler and petty crook who had already served several periods in jail. He was a little man, shorter than average, bald, with thick eyebrows that gave him a permanently startled look. He was bright, silver-tongued, callous, romantic and strong-willed. He was also merciless and possessed a sexual appetite said to be ravenous.

He killed primarily for money, and most of his victims were French widows, women who eeked out a lonely and miserable existence in the years of slaughter from 1914 to 1918, or the depressed years that followed. Each killing followed a similar pattern. Landru placed a notice in the Paris newspapers, advertising himself as a "Widower with two children, with comfortable income, serious and moving in good society", who wished to meet a "widow with a view to matrimony". A meeting would then take place, a relationship would flourish, and then the widow would disappear.

His first five victims perished in his villa at Chantilly, and his career as a killer nearly came to an end before it began. He courted a Mme. Cuchet. They fell out, and Mme. Cuchet asked her family to accompany her to Bluebeard's villa to help achieve reconciliation. When they called, Bluebeard was out, and the family found evidence that Bluebeard was a fraud. Nevertheless, Mme. Cuchet and her young son moved in and were never seen again.

Bluebeard

Henri Desire Landru eloquently but ineffectively proclaims his innocence in court, charged with the murders of eleven women, November 1921.

In 1917 Landru moved to a new villa in Gambais, some 40 kilometres (25 miles) west of Paris. Here he installed a large cast-iron oven, and waited two years, before killing again. It was then that Landru's neighbours in Gambais noticed black, noxious smoke pouring from the chimney of the villa. There were at least five more murders here, but in 1919 Landru's luck-of-the-devil ran out.

A Mlle. Lacoste was searching for her missing sister, Mme. Buisson, last known to be living in a villa in Gambais. Mlle. Lacoste found the villa, but it was deserted. The mayor suggested that she contact the family of a Mme. Collomb, who had also disappeared. The hunt was on, and it was not

long before Mlle. Lacoste spotted Landru coming out of a shop in the area of Paris where murderer and victim had first lived together. Landru was arrested.

It took two years to bring Landru to court, but when he was tried it took the jury only 25 minutes to find him guilty on 11 counts of murder. He was sentenced to the guillotine, and executed in February 1922. On that last morning he declined to hear Mass and refused the traditional glass of brandy from his jailer. Although he had denied all guilt, 50 years after his death, a written confession was discovered, hidden among drawings he had made while in prison.

Some of the victims of Bluebeard: (*opposite, left to right from top row*): Mlle. Marchadier, Mme. Jaume, Mlle. Babelay, Mme. Cruchet, Mme. Laborde, Mme. Colomb, Mme. Buisson, Mme. Pascal, and Mme. Guillin. (*above*) The oven in which Bluebeard was said to have disposed of the bodies of his victims. (*right*) The house in Gambais, where the last of Landru's "wives" were killed.

From 1945 to 1949, the German city of Nuremberg was the setting for the Nuremberg War Trials, an unprecedented series of legal trials to establish the guilt or innocence of leading Nazis on a variety of charges. Never before had the vanquished been brought to book following the end of hostilities, and the choice of Nuremberg was deliberate, for the city was seen by the victors in the World War II as the site of Nazi triumphalism. There were four main crimes covered at Nuremberg: participating in a common plan or conspiring to commit crimes against peace; planning, initiating and waging wars of aggression; war crimes; and crimes against humanity.

Of the 20 or so principal offenders, 12 were sentenced to death though only 10 were in fact executed. Martin Bormann had been sentenced to death in absentia – his remains were accidentally discovered in Berlin in 1972, and it was presumed that he had been shot by Russian snipers on May 1, 1945. Hermann Göring took his own life by poison on the night before he was due to be executed. Those who were executed included three governors of Nazi occupied territories in the war (Hans Frank, Alfred Rosenberg and Arthur Seyss-Inquart); two Nazi ministers (Wilhelm Frick and Joachim von Ribbentrop); and two leading commanders of the Wehrmacht (Alfred Jodl and Wilhelm Keitel) – Jodl was posthumously exonerated by a German de-Nazification court in 1953.

Churchill had wanted such men to be refused a trial and to be summarily executed, but the United States rejected such illegalities. Josef Stalin, the leader of the Soviet Union, advocated the mass execution of some 50,000 to 100,000 German staff officers, but both Churchill and Roosevelt would not countenance this. One American proposal was the Morgenthau Plan, a complete de-nazification of Germany. This was turned down by Stalin. Finally the United States, Britain, France, and the Soviet Union agreed on a series of judicial trials.

Nuremberg Trials

Hermann Göring, the Nazi who cheated the hangman, talks to his lawyer, Dr. Otto Stahmer, March 23, 1946.

Klaus Barbie joined the Nazi Party in 1932, at the age of 19. Three years later he became a member of the *Schutzstaffel*, the notorious SS. After the fall of France, Barbie was appointed head of the Gestapo in Lyon, in the heart of Vichy France. At first he operated from Hotel Terminus, but after a year moved into new headquarters – complete with specially constructed torture chambers – at the Ecole de Santé Militaire. Here he began his career as "The Butcher of Lyon". No one knows how many innocent people Barbie sent to their deaths in the Nazi concentration camps. It is certain, however, that he was responsible for the brutal murder of 44 children at a farm at Izieu, a few miles east of Lyon.

In June 1943, Barbie's Gestapo agents captured Robert Hardy, an activist in the French Resistance. Hardy was tortured but released, possibly so that he might lead the Gestapo to three founder members of the Conseil National de la Résistance: Jean Moulin, Pierre Brossolette, and Charles Delestraint. All three were arrested a fortnight later. Moulin and Brossolette died under torture. Delestraint was sent to Dachau, where he was executed in 1945.

As Allied troops advanced towards Lyon in September 1944, Barbie destroyed all Gestapo records, ordered the killing of hundreds of French civilians who knew about his brutal interrogation methods, and fled to Germany. When the war ended, Barbie was recruited by the U.S. Counter Intelligence Corps. The CIC provided him with a false identity and arranged his passage to Bolivia. Others, with a keener sense of justice, spent the next 36 years hunting for Barbie. In 1983 he was tracked down, extradited by the Bolivian government, and sent to France for trial. Charged in 1987 with the execution or deportation of 842 men, women, and children – a small percentage of his victims – Barbie was found guilty on 341 separate charges, and sentenced to life imprisonment. He died of leukemia in the prison hospital at Lyon in 1991.

Butcher of Lyon

Former SS officer Klaus Barbie reluctantly faces the public outside the Lyon courtroom, May 13, 1987.

On November 17, 1957, Sheriff Arthur Schley and deputies from Plainfield, Wisconsin arrived at a desolate and dilapidated farmhouse. A local hardware store had been robbed, and the owner of the farm had been seen loitering near the store on the day of the robbery. More worrying was that the storeowner, Bernice Worden, had disappeared, and there had been a spate of such disappearances in Wisconsin over the last 10 years.

Sheriff Schley and his men entered the dark farmhouse and were greeted by the overwhelming stench of decomposition and rotting garbage. As they made their way through the rooms something brushed against the Sheriff's jacket. He looked up, to see the headless corpse of Bernice Worden, hanging upside down from one of the beams. The search went on and the horrified lawmen discovered that they had walked into a gruesome madness. There were bowls made from the tops of human skulls, lampshades and wastepaper baskets of human skin, a belt made of nipples, a shoebox full of female genitalia, a collection of noses, an armchair, and even an entire suit made of human skin. They also found Mrs Worden's head, in a burlap sack.

It was all the work of a shy, 51-year-old recluse named Ed Gein. As a young boy, Gein had come to Plainfield in 1914 with his parents George and Augusta, and his older brother Henry. His alcoholic father, deemed worthless by Augusta, had died in 1940 and Henry had died in mysterious circumstances four years later. One night there had been a brush fire dangerously close to the Gein farm. After the fire had been extinguished, Ed Gein had contacted the police to tell them that his brother was missing. Henry's bruised body was found on land untouched by the fire, but the county coroner listed asphyxiation as the cause of death.

Gein was now left with his cold, domineering, verbally-abusive and fanatically religious mother, whom he worshipped. She had always discouraged him from forming friendships and had

Ed Gein

Ed Gein on the day of his arrest in Plainsfield, Wisconsin, November 20, 1957.

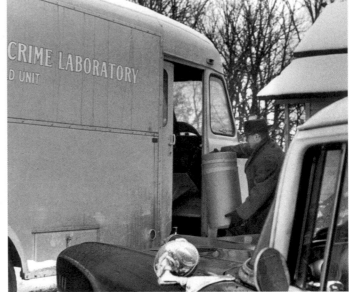

ordered him to have nothing to do with women, but a year after Henry's death, she died after a series of strokes. Gein was shattered. He boarded off the part of the farmhouse she had lived in, keeping it as a shrine, and inhabited just two rooms on the ground floor. Here he became obsessed with accounts he read of head-hunting, exhumation of the dead and the dissection of the human body. He read obituaries in the local paper, and would then visit the graves of recently buried women to plunder their corpses and peel the skin from their bodies. He later told police he never had intercourse with any of these dead women as "they smelled too bad". A semi-retarded friend named Gus accompanied him on these raids, but Gus was moved to an old people's home. It was then that Gein began killing.

Sheriff Schley's men carried out an exhaustive search of the farm and found the remains of 10 women, but nothing to link Gein to their deaths. After days of interrogation, Gein admitted to shooting Bernice Worden and to only one other murder, that of Mary Hogan, the owner of a Plainfield tavern, who had disappeared three years earlier.

The farm became a "museum for the morbid", with one unscrupulous entrepreneur charging 50 cents per head for a guided tour until it burned down on March 20, 1958. Gein's Ford sedan, in which he transported his grisly souvenirs from graveyard to the farm, was put on display in a

(top) The house of horror where Gein lived. (top right) Police scene-of-crime vehicles at Gein's house, November 1957. (above) Visitors in search of the macabre and grisly peer through the windows of Gein's house. (opposite) Ed Gein's kitchen, where police made some of the worst of their discoveries.

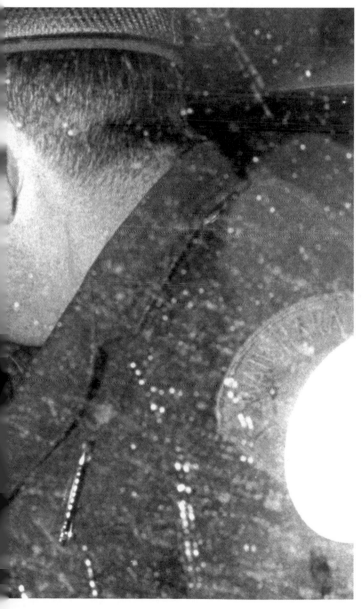

county fair. Children sang songs about Gein, jokes called "Geiners" were bandied about, local people shared what information they had – real or otherwise – with hungry reporters.

As for Gein himself, he was pronounced mentally incompetent, which meant that he could not be tried for first degree murder. He was committed to the Central State Hospital in Waupan, Wisconsin. Ten years later, he was declared fit to stand trial for the murder of Bernice Worden. He was ultimately found "not guilty" by virtue of insanity and sent back to the Central State Hospital. Here he lived out the rest of his life as a model patient, reading voraciously and playing with his ham radio receiver. He died of cancer on 26 July 1984, and was buried next to his mother in the Plainfield cemetery that he had so often visited.

(opposite and above, left to right) Earl Kileen, the District Attorney in charge of the Gein case; a neighboring farmer who employed Gein; Ed Marolla, editor of *The Sun* and a man who investigated the horrific case; Charles Wilson, Head of the Crime Lab; more of Ed Gein's neighbors; the funeral of Bernice Worden. *(left)* The killings come to an end – Ed Gein sits in a police car after his arrest.

Charles Starkweather was born with a mild birth defect called *Genu varum* which caused his legs to be misshapen. He also had a slight speech impediment. Neither was a serious condition in itself, but they did lead to Starkweather being habitually bullied at school. In the school gym he built up his muscles and learned how to take care of himself, and the bullying stopped. It was not until he was in his teens, however, that it was discovered that he suffered from myopia, so severe that he was almost blind, and it was not until he had killed 11 people in two months that his friends and family recognized the destructive power of his inferiority complex.

The killing started late on the night of November 30, 1957. Starkweather drove to a gas station where the attendant refused to sell him a toy dog on credit. Starkweather drove away and then returned with a shotgun. Starkweather took $100 from the till. There was a scuffle. The attendant fell to the floor and Starkweather shot him in the head. He then went to see his girlfriend, Caril Ann Fugate, telling her about the robbery but claiming someone else had killed the attendant.

On January 28, Starkweather was back at Caril's house, where he shot her mother and stepfather, and then strangled Caril's two-year-old sister. Caril witnessed all three killings. The two remained in the house for a few days, with a notice pinned to the front door that warned people to stay away as "Everybody is sick with the Flue". Caril's grandmother became suspicious and called the police, but by the time they arrived Starkweather and Caril had left.

There followed a killing spree in which seven people were shot or stabbed to death by Starkweather. Over 1,200 police officers and members of the National Guard were involved in the hunt, and the two young fugitives were finally captured in Douglas, Wyoming. Starkweather was electrocuted on June 25, 1959. He was 20 years old.

Charles Starkweather

Charles Starkweather, the teenager who went on a killing spree which cost him his life, awaits his nemesis in jail, 1959.

From the summer of 1962 to January 1964, the city of Boston, Massachusetts was terrorized by a series of murders. All the victims were women, all had also been raped or sexually assaulted, and several had been beaten, stabbed, or bitten. In some cases there were ritualistic elements in the way the corpse was left by the killer. The body of the Boston Strangler's last victim – killed on January 4, 1964 – had been stripped and a New Year's Day greetings card had been placed by her left foot.

This was the last killing, but there were two further attacks perpetrated by the man the police believed was the Strangler. In February 1964, his chosen victim proved to be strong enough to fight him off, but was so traumatized by her ordeal that she suffered partial memory loss and was unable to give the police a description of her attacker. Eight months later, however, another young woman was sexually assaulted in Cambridge, just a few miles from Boston. From details she gave them, the police identified Albert de Salvo, a known criminal, as a likely suspect. They arrested him, although they had no idea at the time that he might be the Boston Strangler.

De Salvo was sent to the Boston State Hospital for observation, at the end of which it was decided that he was not mentally fit to stand trial. The authorities were then considerably shaken when de Salvo confessed to being the Strangler. He supplied them with plenty of evidence – details of the murders, sketches of the homes where they had taken place, and even demonstrations of how to tie the knot used in the killings. Frustratingly, however, it was the only evidence that the police had, for the killer had never left any fingerprints. In sum, the police had no real case to present. The state then made a deal with de Salvo's defense team whereby no charges of murder would be brought against him, but he would be prosecuted for the other crimes he had committed.

Boston Strangler

Albert de Salvo, believed to have been the Boston Strangler, genuflects in the chapel at Walpole State Prison, Massachusetts.

The trial began on June 30, 1966 with intense media coverage for its time and with worldwide attention. De Salvo was found guilty as charged and was sentenced to life imprisonment. This proved to be a comparatively short life, for seven years later, he was stabbed to death by a fellow inmate at Walpole State Prison.

Relatives of some of the victims have never accepted that de Salvo was indeed the Strangler. DNA tests carried out in 2001 certainly cast doubt on de Salvo's guilt, and there are claims that another man, regarded by the police as their chief suspect back in 1964 before de Salvo's surprise confession, was the true Strangler.

(*above, left to right*) An undercover police officer on the streets of Boston during the period of the killings. Beacon Hill at dusk – one of the Strangler's hunting grounds. A frightened woman barricades the alley to the rear of her Boston home.

Chicago has known plenty of crime in its history, but the killings that took place on the South Side on the night of July 13–14, 1966 were the worst in the great city's history. Two patrolmen arrived at a nurses' residence at 6:00 A.M. on July 14 to find a young Filipino nurse named Corazon Amurcao standing on a window ledge, screaming with shock and fear, for eight of her colleagues in the same residence had been strangled or stabbed to death (in some cases both) in the past seven hours. The patrolmen calmed the nurse, who then managed to give them a description of the man responsible.

He was about 25 years old, short hair, wearing dark trousers and a dark jacket over a white T shirt. He had smelt of alcohol and had been armed with a gun and a knife. He had claimed that he only wished to rob the nurses, but Corazon had not believed him. When he herded all the nurses from one floor of the residence together, and tied up and gagged them, Corazon crawled under a bunk bed and hid there. She watched in horror as the intruder took the nurses out of the room, one by one, ostensibly so that they would show him where they kept their money or valuables. Corazon noticed that when he returned, he was always alone.

When the police examined the bodies, they discovered that none had been sexually assaulted. They also discovered that the intruder was skilled at tying knots. This led them to a nearby branch of the National Maritime Union, where they were told that Corazon's description matched a man named Richard Speck, who had been at the Union seeking work a couple of days earlier. Detectives now visited bars, clubs, and hotels. They struck lucky at the Raleigh Hotel, where Speck was registered, and where they found the clothes that Corazon had described. They also found fingerprints that matched those at the nurses' residence. Two days later they were called to the Starr Hotel where Speck had slashed his wrists. The following April, Speck was sentenced to death, the sentence being commuted to terms of imprisonment of 400 years.

Richard Speck

Richard Speck, accused of murdering eight nurses in a single night, arrives at court in the winter of 1966.

Early in 1979 the Chicago police found the bodies of 28 young men beneath the home of 37-year-old John Wayne Gacy in the affluent suburb of Des Plaines. Gacy confessed to killing them all, and told the police he had thrown five more corpses into nearby rivers when he ran out of space beneath the house. He had attempted to speed up the decomposition process with the use of chemicals. The stench from the remains was horrendous.

At the beginning of the 1970s Gacy had spent 18 months of a 10 year sentence in prison after being convicted of sodomy. He was known to be an aggressive man with mental problems. He had been cruelly treated by his father as a child, and had suffered blackouts after being hit by a playground swing at the age of 11. He also had a heart condition. Given all this, it was surprising that he had been able to overcome his victims, all of whom were in the prime of life, but Gacy had a most vicious trick.

In his spare time he did charity work, dressing up as Pogo the Clown and performing for children in hospital. Once he had persuaded a potential victim to come to his house, Gacy would show them a pair of handcuffs that he said he used in his act as Pogo. He said they were trick cuffs, and invited his guest to put them on. The trick was that the cuffs were genuine. Once the victim was securely manacled, Gacy beat them or chloroformed them, then stripped and raped them, sometimes torturing and even garroting them.

The horrific career came to and end in 1978 with the disappearance of a young man last seen in Gacy's company. Police searched his house, but found nothing – and accepted that the ghastly smell came from a cracked sewage pipe. A second search, however, revealed the grim truth. On May 9, 1994 Gacy was executed by lethal injection.

John Wayne Gacy

The police photograph of John Wayne Gacy taken shortly after his arrest, December 21, 1978.

POLICE DEPT.
DES PLAINES, ILL.
7.8..4.6.2.12-21-78

On the evening of November 14, 1974 police were called to a house in Amityville, Suffolk County, New York. There they discovered six dead bodies – the entire DeFeo family save one. Mother and father, two brothers and two sisters had been shot with a high-powered rifle as they slept in their beds. The only survivor, Ronald Junior (known as Butch), appeared distraught. When questioned, he suggested that the man responsible might be Louis Fatini, a Mafia mobster whom Butch claimed had a grudge against his father.

There were problems with this story. Butch was a hot-tempered young man, a drug addict with a known interest in firearms – he had once turned a loaded shotgun on one of his best friends. More to the point, on more than one occasion he had threatened to kill his father – the last occasion being less than a week before the killings. Although Butch provided a detailed alibi, some of it did not make sense.

Eventually the truth emerged. Early on the morning of November 14, Butch had taken his .35 caliber Martin rifle, gone to his parents' bedroom and fired two shots into his father, two shots into his mother. He had then moved on to his brothers' bedroom and killed both John and Mark with a single shot each. Finally he had entered the room where his sisters slept and killed them.

At his trial a year later, Butch's counsel had attempted to enter a plea of insanity. Butch told the court: "When I get a gun in my hand, there's no doubt in my mind who I am. I am God." There was clear evidence, however, that in the aftermath of the killing he had acted with considerable cunning – throwing his own bloodstained clothes down a storm drain was not considered by the jury to be the action of a madman. He was found guilty and sentenced to 25 years to life on all six counts of murder.

Amityville Horror

The pretty house in which Ronald DeFeo Junior shot six members of his family in a single night. It was subsequently said to be haunted.

As a child Ted Bundy lived with his mother and grandmother, passed off by both of them as his mother's "brother". As a young man he was to enter the world of the petty criminal – thieving, shoplifting, and using his considerable charm to con his fellow citizens. Tragically there was a darker side to his character which emerged when Bundy was 28 years old and living in Seattle. In the early hours of January 5, 1974 Bundy broke into the basement bedroom of Joni Lopez, a student at the University of Washington, bludgeoned her with a crowbar and left her lying in a pool of blood. Thereafter she suffered from serious brain damage. Over the next 10 months Bundy killed 10 women in and around Seattle before moving on to Utah.

The killing continued wherever he went. On October 18, Bundy raped, sodomized, and killed a 17-year-old girl. Three weeks later, posing as a policeman, he lured a woman into his car and attempted to handcuff her. She managed to struggle free, wrench open the car door, escape, and give descriptions of Bundy and his car to the police. Nine months later Bundy's car was recognized and he was arrested. He was sentenced to 15 years imprisonment.

His murderous past now caught up with him. He was put on trial for his earlier killings. During a court recess Bundy, who conducted his own defense, was allowed to visit the courthouse library. He jumped from the second-story window and remained at large for a week. Back in jail he used a hacksaw blade to cut a hole in the ceiling of his cell, climbed out and walked free. With $500 in his pocket (somehow smuggled in to him) he bought a plane ticket to Chicago and eventually made his way to Florida where he attacked six more women, killing three of them.

On July 31, 1979 Bundy was sentenced to death. He spent almost 10 years on Death Row until the end came on January 24, 1989. His last meal was steak, fried eggs, and hash browns. His last words were: "Give my love to my family and friends", before he was electrocuted.

Ted Bundy

Ted Bundy takes time out from killing in 1975 to do the dishes. Although he claimed to be socially inept, he had good looks and a genial manner that he used to lure his victims into his VW car.

For almost exactly a year, from July 1976 to July 1977, the citizens of the Bronx, Queens and Long Island were terrorized by a series of shootings. The victims were almost always couples sitting in a parked car – exceptionally one victim was shot while walking home on her own – and there was no discernible motive in any case. These were random killings and woundings by a madman.

Police Captain Joseph Borelli believed that they were the work of a woman-hater, but a letter found at the scene of an attack in April 1977 denied this. It was from the killer himself, who appeared deeply hurt by Borelli's suggestion. "I am not a woman-hater. But I am a monster. I am the Son of Sam..." A note from the killer to a New York newspaper used the same title, and has gone down in the annals of crime.

The Son of Sam indulged himself in just two more shootings – on June 26 and July 31, 1977. In the first a young couple were both shot and wounded; in the second the woman was killed, the man blinded. But the Son of Sam now made a mistake. When he returned to his own car from the last shooting, he found a parking ticket on the windscreen. A woman walking her dog nearby noticed that he tore up the ticket and threw it away. She also noticed that he had a gun.

The police traced the owner of the car – a young postal-worker named David Berkowitz. He lived on his own in Yonkers and had deep seated feelings of persecution. Berkowitz was also reckoned to be mentally ill. He claimed that he heard voices of demons telling him to kill. He also said that after killing he felt "flushed with power".

He was, however, judged to be sane and was sentenced to 365 years imprisonment.

Son of Sam

The police mug shot of David Berkowitz, the New York City serial killer who called himself "Son of Sam".

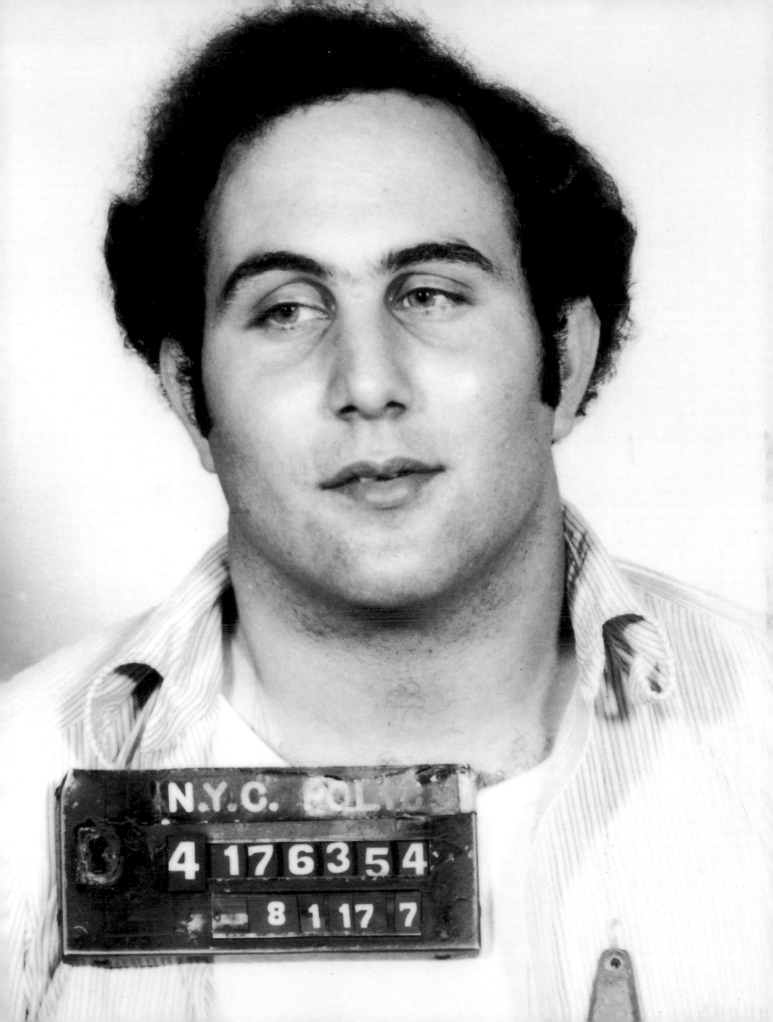

Between November 1 and November 29, 1977, members of the Los Angeles police found the bodies of eight women dumped on curbsides or hillsides in and around the city. All were between 12 and 28 years old, all had been strangled, some were naked. Another body was discovered on December 13 and two months later the 10th victim of what the press had dubbed the "Hillside Strangler" was found in the trunk of a Datsun.

Early in the investigation the police made two important deductions: more than one killer was involved; and whoever was responsible knew the city well. In January 1979 the bodies of two female students were found in an abandoned car near Bellingham. One of them was known to have recently agreed to house-sit for a security guard named Kenneth Bianchi. Bianchi had moved to Bellingham from Los Angeles, where he had lived for a while with his cousin Angelo Buono. Police suspected that the two men were jointly the Hillside Strangler. They were an odd pair. Bianchi was good-looking, while Buono was surly, ignorant and sadistic – he had raped his 14-year-old stepdaughter. The two men had needed money back in 1977, so they had forced two young women into prostitution and bought a list of possible clients from two streetwalkers, Deborah Noble and Yolanda Washington. Yolanda became their first murder victim.

Bianchi made a deal with the state. He would implicate Buono if he could be tried and imprisoned in California – where he would get life, rather than in Washington, where he would be sentenced to death. Once in jail, however, Bianchi changed his mind. In a weird development, a woman named Veronica Compton, who had fallen in love with Bianchi, now agreed to go to Washington and commit a similar murder, thereby casting doubt on Buono and Bianchi's guilt. She failed to kill her intended victim, was arrested and imprisoned. The trials of the two Hillside Stranglers took well over two years. Both were sentenced to life. Buono died in Calipatria State Prison on September 21, 2002.

Hillside Stranglers

The leading figure in the a series of horrific murders during the late 1970s – Kenneth Bianchi, the Hillside Strangler.

Like other serial killers who have worked in hospitals or clinics, Donald Harvey repeatedly found himself in a position from which he could dispense death. He has repeatedly averred that the lives he took were "mercy killings", that he killed to prevent pain and suffering, but the facts behind most of the 15 murders for which he has been convicted do not fit that pattern. In several cases he killed, or attempted to kill out of spite or hatred.

As a teenager, Harvey was too bright to be anything but bored at High School, and he quit education at the age of 16. Marymount was the first hospital at which he found work, and quite why he suddenly began to kill remains a mystery. Harvey own account of his first murder refers to a stroke victim rubbing faeces on his face. "The next thing I knew, I'd smothered him," Harvey told the *Cincinnati Post* 27 years after the event. There were more occasional killings at Marymount until Harvey joined the Air Force in 1971.

In September 1975, Harvey got a job at the Cincinnati VA Medical Hospital and over the next 10 years murdered 15 or more patients there. He kept precise records of the methods used in these killings: by poisoning, by asphyxiation, or by injecting cyanide into an intravenous tube or directly into a patient's buttocks.

But it was cyanide that eventually led to his arrest. During an autopsy on a patient who had unexpectedly died at the Cincinnati Drake Memorial Hospital, the coroner noted a faint smell of almonds, often an indication of the presence of cyanide. A list of those people who had access to the patient included Harvey's name.

He was convicted of 15 murders in all. His first parole hearing is set for 2047 when Harvey will be 95 years old.

Angel of Death

Donald Harvey, known as the "Angel of Death", appears in court at Cincinnati, August 1987. He pleaded guilty to 24 charges of aggravated murder and four charges of attempted murder. He was described by those who knew him in childhood as "a loner and teacher's pet".

In April 2001, the new Sheriff of King County, Washington decided it was time to take a fresh look at what had become known as the Case of the Green River Killer. Some 20 years had elapsed since the first bodies had been fished out of the Green River, and the number of the killer's victims was now reckoned to be almost 50. Previous investigations had cost $15 million, had produced plenty of suspects, but had failed to find any real evidence as to who was responsible. The Sheriff assembled a task-force devoted to the hunt for the Green River Killer. Others had tried before, but this time technology came to the rescue of the forces of law and order.

Samples of the semen found in the bodies of three victims killed in the early 1980s were sent for DNA testing. They were compared with similar samples taken from one of the earlier suspects, a middle-aged truck painter named Gary Ridgway. When news reached the Sheriff that the samples matched, he burst into tears. An appalling nightmare was about to end.

The vast majority of Ridgway's victims were prostitutes. Ridgway was obsessed by prostitutes, hating them, reviling them but always cruising around the areas where they were to be found. He would pick them up in one of the several trucks he owned, drive them to a remote place, and kill them – usually by strangulation. He would then take their bodies to one of his "dumping grounds", one of his favorites being the Green River. It was here that the search for the killer began back in 1982, when, on a hot summer's day, a man fishing in the Green River had come across two bodies in the shallows.

Ridgway has confessed to 48 murders, but police in Washington, Oregon, California, and British Columbia believe that he may well have killed many other women. There are even theories that there was more than one Green River Killer.

Green River Killer

Gary Ridgway leaves the King County Washington
Superior Courtroom after receiving 48 life sentences,
December 18, 2003.

Henry Lee Lucas presented himself as the most prolific killer of all time, claiming to have murdered some 3,000 people between 1975 and 1983 – a rate of approximately a murder a day. On another occasion, he put the figure at perhaps 350 killings, but even that is likely to be a huge exaggeration. When he was arrested in 1983 he was charged with only two murders, although a special Task Force appointed to handle his case believed they could close another 213 murder files following Lucas's mass confessions.

He was born in 1936. His father was an ex-railroad worker who had lost both legs in an accident. His mother was a prostitute, a violent woman who beat Lucas regularly. Lucas claimed to have first killed at the age of 15, strangling a young girl who refused his sexual advances. He later retracted this claim. He did a little time for burglary in the late 1950s, and then killed his mother on January 11, 1960, stabbing her to death when she attacked him.

He served 15 years and was released in 1975. Lucas then drifted to Florida where he teamed up with a man named Otis Toole, with whom Lucas alleged he committed "hundreds" of murders. He was arrested in June 1983 for firearms violation, and then charged on two counts of murder, an 82-year-old woman in Ringgold, Texas, and Toole's young niece Frieda Powell.

The evidence against him was not strong, but Lucas pleaded guilty, stating in open court that he had "killed about 100 more women". He often later produced reasons for these staggering confessions, such that he was trying to get better treatment. Certainly Lucas received treatment far different from that accorded most prisoners. He was not chained or handcuffed. He was sometimes given the number code to open doors inside his prison. He was occasionally taken out to eat in cafes or restaurants. Lucas was convicted of eleven murders and sentenced to death. This was commuted to life imprisonment. He died in prison of heart failure in March 2001.

Henry Lee Lucas

A police photo of Henry Lee Lucas. At the time he was under sentence of death, but this was later uniquely commuted by the then Governor of Texas George W. Bush.

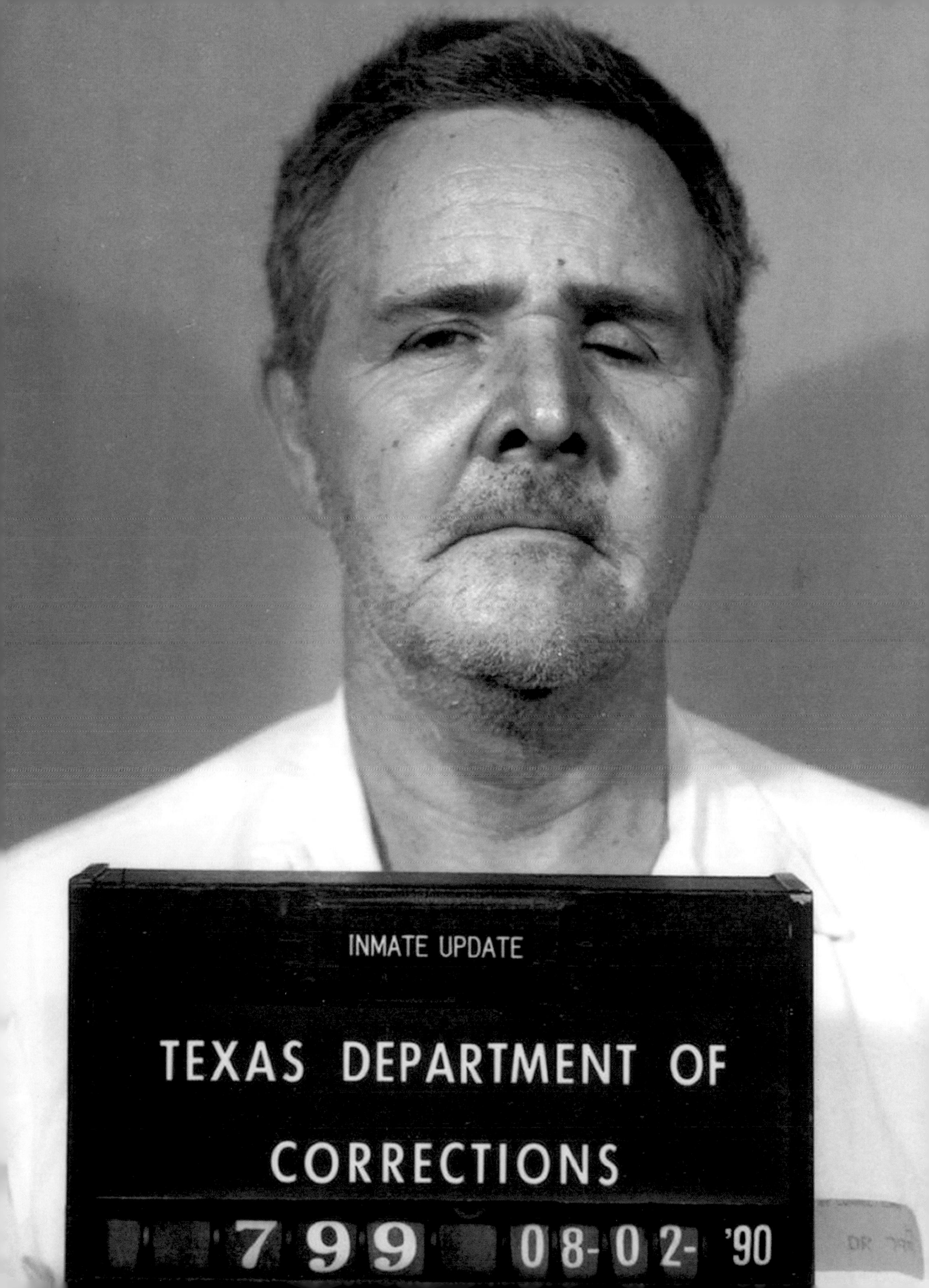

INMATE UPDATE

TEXAS DEPARTMENT OF

CORRECTIONS

7 99   08-02- '90

A dolfo Constanzo was only 26 when he died, shot at his own request by a professional hit-man named El Duby while hiding from the police in a small apartment in Mexico City. Constanzo's life had been one that mixed drugdealing with magic and voodoo, fortune-telling with fortune-making. He was born in 1962, the son of a teenage Cuban immigrant named Aurora Constanzo. She later moved with young Adolfo to Little Havana in Miami, and here she intro-duced him to the practice of voodoo (*palo mayombe*). As a teenager he became involved in petty crime. In 1984 he moved to Mexico City, where he set up his fortune-telling business and offered ritual cleansings, with a price list for sacrificial beasts: roosters $6, goats $30, boa constrictors $450. For a higher price, he offered to make local drug dealers bullet-proof.

In 1985, Constanzo and his disciples raided a nearby graveyard for human bones, so that they could start their own *nganga* – the traditional cauldron of blood used in *palo mayombe*. As well as drug dealers, Constanzo now numbered among his clients, models, night-club performers, and police officers, but it was the dealers who brought in the most money. By 1987, Constanzo had a luxury apartment and a fleet of cars including an $80,000 Mercedes. The magic was working well, but the *nganga* needed human blood, and Constanzo and others embarked on a series of ritual human killings.

Police fished the remains of victims from the Zumpango River – corpses without ears, feet, fingers, hearts, genitalia, and brains. The rituals became more elaborate and more sadistic, and Constanzo became more reckless, taking on top drug dealers, executing them and dumping their bodies on the street. It couldn't last. On May 6, 1989 neighbors complained of noise coming from Constanzo's hideaway apartment. Police surrounded the block, and Constanzo called for El Duby to do his work.

Mexican Voodoo

Sergio Martinez, one of the many members of Adolfo Constanzo's voodoo brotherhood, exhumes a victim's body while the police take pictures, April 1989.

There was little in Aileen Wuornos's 46 years of life that was not shot through with pain and suffering, despair, and hardship. As a young girl she had no contact with her father, who committed suicide in prison when Aileen was 13 years old. Her mother abandoned her, and she was brought up by her grandparents. Her grandmother was an abusive alcoholic, her grandfather was a bully who physically abused and assaulted her. When they discovered that 14-year-old Aileen was pregnant, they threw her out of the house. Her baby boy was put up for adoption.

In late September 1976 Aileen hitch-hiked to Florida, getting a ride from a 69-year-old Yacht Club president named Lewis Fell whom she subsequently married. However, the ride was ultimately to prove a fatal journey. Twenty years later, under Governor Jeb Bush, Florida was enthusiastically pursuing a policy of carrying out the death sentence. The marriage to Fell lasted only a month or two, and in 1981 Aileen was arrested for armed robbery. She spent 13 months in prison, but was back within less than a year, for passing forged checks.

Her crimes became more frequent and more serious – grand theft auto, demanding with menaces, making threatening phone calls. For a year she found some happiness with a gay lover, but Wuornos had to work as a prostitute to support the pair of them. The romance died and as the hard times bit harder, Aileen became more desperate. On November 30, 1989 she killed for the first time. In less than 12 months she killed five more times.

When she came to trial, she pleaded guilty to all but one of the murders, claiming that in the case of her first killing she had been acting in self-defense. She received six death sentences. She declined the traditional "last meal", but instead took a cup of coffee. Her last words were: "I'm sailing with the Rock… and I'll be back with Jesus…"

Aileen Wuornos

A Florida Department of Corrections photograph of
Aileen Wuornos, taken toward the end of her life.

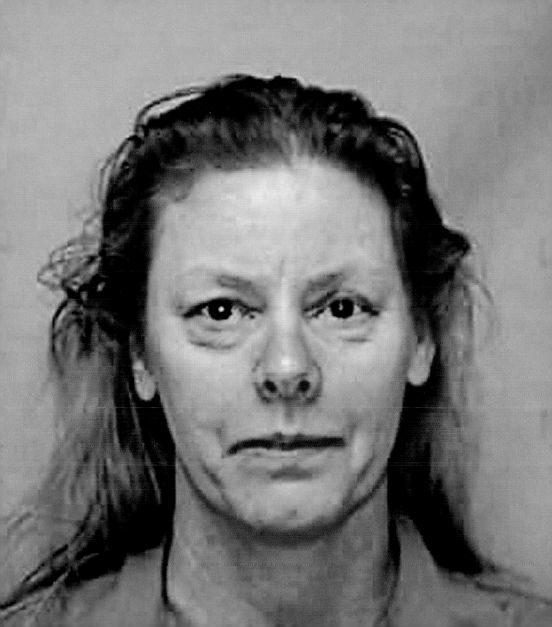

Andrei Chikatilo was born on October 16, 1936 in Yablochnoye, a village in the heart of the Ukraine. It was a tough time in a tough place – an older brother had vanished five years earlier, and Andrei's parents feared that he had been eaten by starving neighbors. Such fears may well have had a profound psychological effect on young Andrei. In 1941 the Nazi invasion of the USSR and the Ukraine led to Andrei's village being overrun by German troops. It is thought that the little boy may well have witnessed appalling atrocities. He was a weak youth, short-sighted, a chronic bedwetter, lonely and painfully shy.

For a while he coped with life – serving in the army, getting a job as a telephone engineer, marrying and raising two children. Then he got a job as a schoolteacher and began to abuse both boys and girls. He was forced to resign, but no other action was taken, so it was not until Andrei was in his early forties that he first killed. This was the dreadful murder of a nine-year-old girl whom Andrei blindfolded, unsuccessfully attempted to rape, stabbed three times, and then, while she was still alive, threw into a bitterly cold river. Andrei was arrested, but was released when his wife provided him with a false alibi.

Three and a half years later he killed again. His victim was a local Rostov girl with a reputation for having "loose morals". He led her to some dense woodland, where he stripped, punched, and strangled her, filling her mouth with earth so that she could not scream. This time Andrei was excited by what he had done. A year later he killed again, and then killed six more times in the next 12 months.

A Moscow detective was sent to Rostov to handle the case. It was believed that a single sex-crazed killer, whom they called the Forest Strip killer, was responsible for what now amounted to

Rostov Ripper

30 of the known victims murdered and cannibalized by Andrei Chikatilo between 1978 and 1990.

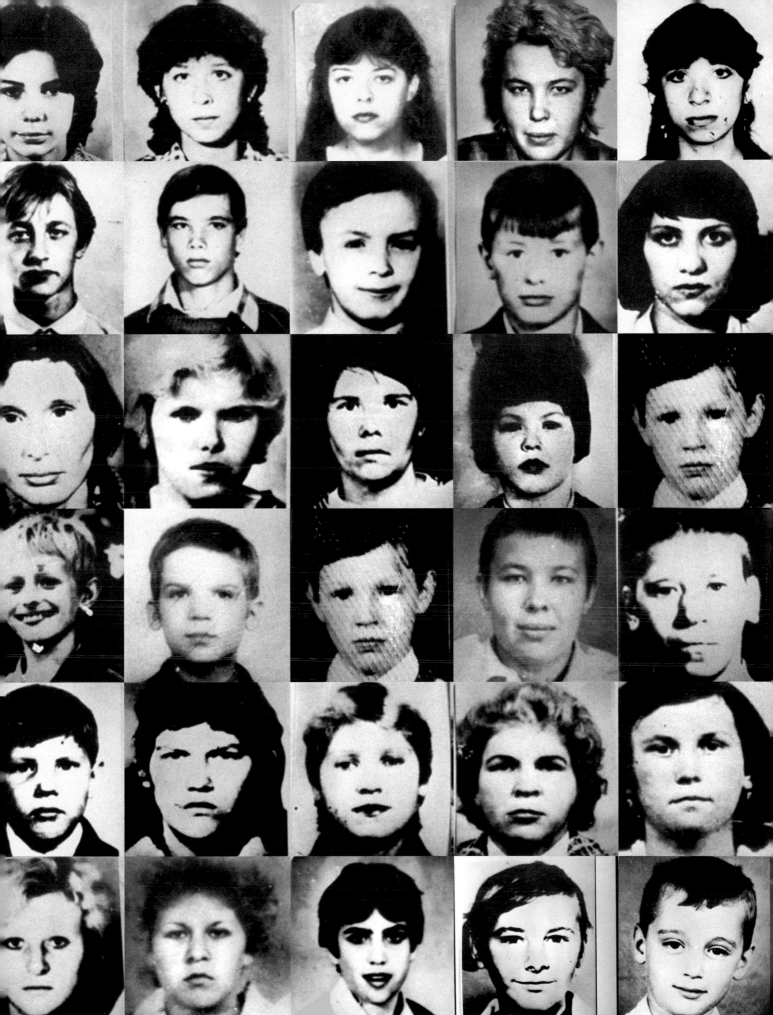

(*top*) Police photographs of Chikatilo taken following his final arrest. (*opposite bottom*) The black leather bag used by Chikatilo to carry the gruesome tools of his trade – a knife, a length of rope. and a jar of lubricant. (*opposite top*) The man who tracked down the Red Ripper – Homicide Chief Viktor Burakov surveys the mountain of paperwork left in the Ripper's wake.

14 murders, though the term "serial killer" was never used – such a phenomenon existed only in the degenerate, capitalist West. Andrei was suspected and arrested, but released when the results of a DNA test were wrongly interpreted. A year passed, and then a Rostov police inspector saw Andrei hanging around the bus station and approaching young girls. He was arrested on suspicion, but again released. He went on killing.

When he was finally brought to trial in 1992 he was convicted of 52 murders. In 1994 he was executed by a single bullet fired into the back of his head.

The man who became known as the BTK Strangler was born in 1945. He was Dennis Lynn Rader, an ex-supermarket worker and security guard with a bachelor's degree in Administration of Justice. The "justice" that Rader himself administered was both summary and horrific, for the letters BTK were his own private code for "bind them, torture them, kill them". He described his victims as "projects", the act of killing as "putting them down", and referred to his weapons and equipment as his "hit kit" – it contained guns, tape, rope, and handcuffs.

Between 1974 and 1991, he killed 10 people from Wichita – men, women, and children. His pre-ferred method was strangulation, although in one case he stabbed his victim to death. He took time and trouble over his killings, identifying his victims and then stalking them until he had got to know their routines and the patterns of their daily lives. His method was then to wait until the victim was away from home, break in, cut the telephone line, and wait for the victim's return. Death was seldom quick. Rader strangled his victims, let them recover, then strangled them again, repeating this process until he became sexually aroused.

For over 30 years Rader successfully avoided detection, until March 2004 when he began to send letters to relatives of his victims, the *Wichita Eagle*, the local police, and Wichita's KAKE-TV station. These letters were poorly spelt and ungrammatical, but contained information about the killings. On February 25, 2005 he was arrested by Wichita police. He claimed that he had chosen to risk giving himself away partly because his own children had grown up and he was bored, and also so that his arrest might coincide with the publication of a book called *Nightmare in Wichita – the Hunt for the BTK Strangler* by Robert Beattie. Four months later he pleaded guilty to 10 counts of first-degree murder, giving graphic and detailed accounts of his own bes-tiality. He received 10 consecutive life sentences without the possibility of parole for 175 years.

BTK Strangler

One of the masks worn by the BTK Killer is held up in court by a police detective, August 18, 2005.

On July 22, 1991 two police officers were driving through a run-down area of Milwaukee when they saw a black man with a single handcuff attached to his wrist staggering along the street. He led them to an apartment at 924 North 25th Street belonging to Jeffrey Dahmer, a 31-year-old white. Dahmer opened the door and explained that a bit of drunken foolery had got out of hand. He went to his bedroom to get the key to the handcuffs. One of the officers followed him, and noticed dozens of photographs of dismembered bodies and human skulls inside a refrigerator.

Coming out of the bedroom into the kitchen area, he recognized the same refrigerator, opened it, and screamed. It contained a complete human head. Dahmer was arrested and a thorough search was made of the apartment. The horrified searchers found more human heads, hands, and penises in a stockpot, human meat in a freezer, jars of preserved genitalia, chloroform, and perhaps the most macabre collection of photographs ever assembled.

Dahmer had killed his first victim while still a student in high school back in 1978 – a young hitch-hiker he had picked up near Akron, Ohio. Over the next nine years he had kept his murderous impulses in check, but in September 1987 he killed again. In his last month of freedom, Dahmer was killing at the rate of one victim a week. By the time he was arrested, he had killed 17 people, all male, all black, all young, all bisexual or homosexual. His method was to invite the victim back to his apartment, give them a spiked drink or chloroform them, then strangle them or stab them to death.

The skulls and preserved items that the police found in his apartment he regarded as "trophies". The flesh in the freezer was meat. The rest of the remains were boiled down with chemicals and

Jeffrey Dahmer

The Milwaukee Cannibal is brought to justice. Jeffrey Dahmer enters the courtroom on August 6, 1991.

Dahmer's neighbor, Mrs Vernell Bass, indicates the apartment where Dahmer killed and cannibalized 11 of his victims, July 27, 1991. By then the refrigerator and freezer had mercifully been removed.

acids and poured away. The stench from such operations was overpowering. But Dahmer also performed his own gruesome experiments. He performed lobotomies on some of his unconscious victims. In one case he is said to have drilled a hole in the skull of a man and poured a solution of hydrochloric acid into it. The poor man lived for several days in a zombie-like state.

At his trial he was protected by an 18-foot high barrier. His plea of guilty but insane was brushed aside, and he was sentenced to 957 years. He served only two before being murdered by a fellow inmate. To avoid the obscenity of any Dahmer Collection being created, the city of Milwaukee raised $400,000 to buy Dahmer's tools, photographs and refrigerator, all of which were then destroyed.

Assassination

The President of Egypt, Anwar al-Sadat, is assassinated
by an armed group of Islamic fundamentalists during a
military parade in Cairo on October 6, 1981.

On April 9, 1865, General Robert E. Lee, in immaculate white uniform, surrendered to a mud-spattered General Ulysses S. Grant at Appomattox, Virginia. The War Between the States was finally over, but intense bitterness remained. For President Abraham Lincoln the great task ahead was to bring real peace to a divided nation. On April 14 he made one last speech on the subject of Amnesty and Reconciliation, declaring that the Confederate states should be returned to "their proper practical relation with the Union as quickly as possible". The President then decided to take the evening off and visit a performance of *Our American Cousin* at Ford's Theater in Washington D.C.

Unknown to the President or the authorities, for over three months a group of conspirators had been planning to kidnap Lincoln and hold him hostage against the release of Confederate prisoners of war. Now the war was over, there was no point in kidnapping the President, and the conspirators changed their plan to one of simultaneously murdering Lincoln and members of his cabinet. Their leader, an actor named John Wilkes Booth, visited Ford's Theater on the morning of the April 14 and learned of Lincoln's intended visit. The conspirators hurriedly met at a boarding house owned by Mary Surratt and decided that while Booth dealt with Lincoln, George Atzerodt was to kill the Vice-President Andrew Johnson, and Lewis Paine and David Herold would kill the Secretary of State William Seward. The murders were to take place at 10:15 P.M.

Lincoln and his wife, with their friends Clara Harris and Henry Rathbone, arrived at Ford's at 8:30 P.M. Booth arrived an hour later, told William Burroughs, a boy who worked at the theater, to mind his horse in the rear alley, and then went to the next-door saloon to fortify himself with a drink. He entered the theater at 10:07 P.M. He knew Ford's well and had no difficulty making his way to the State Box. Here he was in luck. Lincoln's bodyguard, John Parker of the Metropolitan

Lincoln Assassination

John Wilkes Booth, the man who killed President Abraham Lincoln.

Police Force, had temporarily left his post. Drawing his single shot Derringer and a hunting knife, Booth entered the box, shot Lincoln in the back of the head at point blank range, stabbed Rathbone in the arm, and leapt 11 feet (3.3 metres) to the stage below. As he landed, he broke his left fibula just above the ankle. In front of an audience of more than a 1,000 people, while Mrs Lincoln screamed, Booth flashed his knife and shouted "Thus always to tyrants!". He then limped to the back door of the theater and galloped away on his horse. A doctor in the theater audience hurried to the President's box. He found that the bullet had entered through Lincon's left ear and lodged behind his right eye. The President was paralysed and hardly able to breathe. He never recovered consciousness and died nine hours later, a little before 7:30 in the morning at the Petersen house, opposite the theater.

Booth rode through the night to Surrattsville. Here he met Herold, and the two rode on to Dr. Samuel Mudd's house, where the doctor set and put a splint on Booth's leg. The following afternoon, Booth and Herold left Mudd's house and headed south. Eleven days later, federal authorities caught up with them at a farm near Port Royal, Virginia. Booth shot himself. Herold surrendered. The other

(*clockwise from top left*) Alexander Gardner's portrait of Lincoln, November 8, 1863. A poster offering $100,000 reward for the capture of Booth. The private box at Ford's Theater at the time of Lincoln's assassination. The conspirators: (right to left) David E. Herold, Michael O'Laughlin, Edman Spangler, Samuel Arnold, George Atzerodt, and Lewis Paine.

A considerable crowd of officials and reporters witness the execution of Mary Surratt (extreme left), Lewis Paine, George Atzerodt, and David Herold, four of the conspirators involved in the assassination of President Lincoln, July 7 1865.

conspirators were rounded up and four of them, Herold, Paine, Atzerodt, and Mary Surratt were hanged on the gallows at the Old Penitentiary on July 7, 1865.

Booth's aim had been to plunge Washington and the Federal Government into chaos, and thereby rekindle the South's fighting spirit. It was all too late. The South had been brought to its knees. The war was already over, and Booth and his companions did little more than prolong

some of the misery and bitterness of its aftermath. As for the plot itself, Atzerodt had failed to make any attempt on the Vice-President's life, and although Paine had twice slashed Secretary Seward's throat, the poor man was saved by an iron surgical collar that he was wearing. Although the capital was stunned and appalled, and Lincoln's death profoundly shocked the nation, business proceeded as usual under Vice-President Johnson's care.

William McKinley was elected President of the United States in 1896, after what is generally considered the first modern-style election campaign. He was something of an imperialist, who led his country into the Spanish–American War, the outcome of which enabled the United States to gain control of much of the northern Caribbean, and secured the annexation of both Hawaii and Wake Island. He was re-elected in 1900.

Early in September 1901 McKinley visited the Pan-American Exposition in Buffalo, New York. On September 5, he was scheduled to address an audience estimated of 50,000. As his carriage drove through the Exposition grounds, bands played, people cheered and pressed round him, wanting to shake his hand. His staff had long warned him of the danger of such an open and friendly approach, but he had always replied "No one would wish to hurt me".

At midday McKinley began his address, speaking of the glory days ahead for the United States, reaching a climax that prompted enormous more cheers, then walking through the vast crowds. Nothing went wrong. He had once again proved to his staff that their fears were groundless.

The following day, after a visit to Niagara Falls, McKinley returned to the Exposition, and at 4:00 P.M. doors to the reception auditorium were thrown open to admit the public. Seven minutes later a young anarchist named Leon Czolgosz stepped forward, as though to shake the President's hand, and fired two rapid shots. One bullet simply bounced off a button on McKinley's coat, but the other passed through his stomach. He was taken to the Exposition temporary hospital, ill-equipped and ill-lit. Surgeons tried to find the bullet, but failed. No one thought to use the new X-ray machine, an exhibit in the nearby Technology Building. McKinley survived for just over a week, rallying at first, but then dying from the gangrene that had set in. His last words were "Nearer, my God, to Thee".

McKinley Assassination

The Man Who Killed the President… Leon Czolgosz
behind bars after shooting William McKinley.

Just before 10:00 A.M. on Sunday, June 28, 1914, Archduke Franz Ferdinand, heir-apparent to the Austro-Hungarian Empire, arrived in the town of Sarajevo. He had come to the capital of Bosnia–Herzegovina to direct army manoeuvres in the nearby mountains. Accompanied by his pregnant wife, the Archduchess Sophia, Franz Ferdinand was in jovial mood. It was good to get away from the stuffy atmosphere of the Imperial court in Vienna, where his wife was not accorded the respect and honor that he felt was due to her. That was because, although Sophia von Chotkovato came from a noble Bohemian family, she had never been considered a suitable wife for Franz Ferdinand. In Austria, she was not permitted to sit at her husband's side in a royal carriage or in the royal box with him at the Opera. Here, in Sarajevo, protocol was different. The Governor, General Oskar Potiorek, had made it clear that the Archduchess would be made most welcome. It would be pleasant for the royal couple to spend the day truly together. They set off, driving through the city in an open car.

The Archduke's good mood lasted precisely 10 minutes. Unknown to Franz Ferdinand and his military escort, nine members of the Narodna Odbrana, a group seeking Bosnian independence, were positioned along the route that the Archduke and Archduchess would take from the railway station to the City Hall, where an official reception awaited them. Long before they reached City Hall, however, an attempt was made to assassinate the imperial couple. As the car passed Nedeljko Cabrinovic, the young nationalist hurled a grenade.

Accounts differ as to precisely what happened. The official version is that the chauffeur of the royal car saw the missile in mid-air, reacted swiftly, and accelerated. The grenade exploded under the wheels of the following car, seriously wounding two of its occupants. The version given by Borijove Jevtic, another of the conspirators, is that the grenade hit the side of Franz

Franz Ferdinand Assassination

The uniform coat worn by the Archduke Franz Ferdinand on the day of his assassination in Sarajevo, June 28, 1914.

(*far left*) In happier times, Franz Ferdinand and the Archduchess Sophia with their children in 1909. (*left*) The Archduke at his reception in Sarajevo, a short while before he was killed. (*below*) Ferdinand and Sophia shortly after their arrival in Sarajevo, June 28, 1914. (*opposite*) One of Princip's fellow conspirators, Nedeljko Cabrinovic, is arrested after his failed attempt to kill the Archduke.

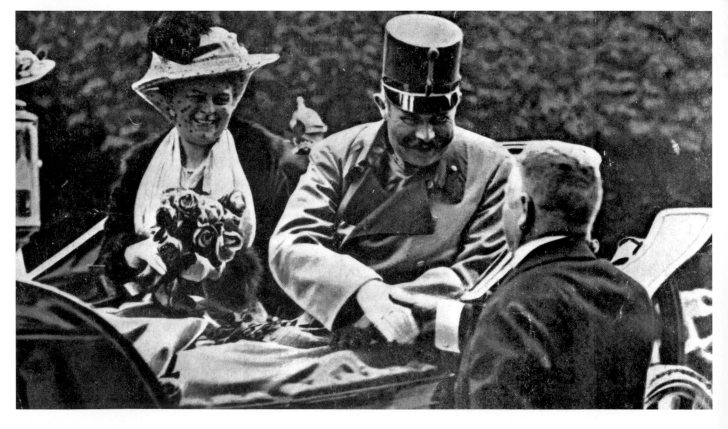

Ferdinand's car, but that the Archduke, with "great presence of mind", threw himself back in the seat and escaped injury. The car drove on at speed to the City Hall.

After attending the reception in the City Hall, Franz Ferdinand asked about the men who had been wounded, and insisted on being taken to see them. A member of the Archduke's staff suggested this might be dangerous, but General Potiorek said: "Do you think Sarajevo is full of assassins?" It was decided that the Archduchess should remain at City Hall, but she refused, saying: "As long as the Archduke shows himself in public today, I shall not leave him".

Unhappily, no one saw fit to inform the chauffeur of the change in plans. He set off expecting to drive to the railway station, not to the hospital. When this became clear, Potiorek shouted to the chauffeur: "What is this? This is the wrong way! We're supposed to take the Appel Quay!" He ordered that the car be turned around. As the poor driver executed a laborious three-point turn, another conspirator, Gavrilo Princip, was passing. He looked up to see the man he and his fellow-conspirators had come to kill sitting in a stationery open car, just a metre or two away from him. Princip drew an automatic pistol from his coat, leapt on to the running board of the car, and fired just two shots.

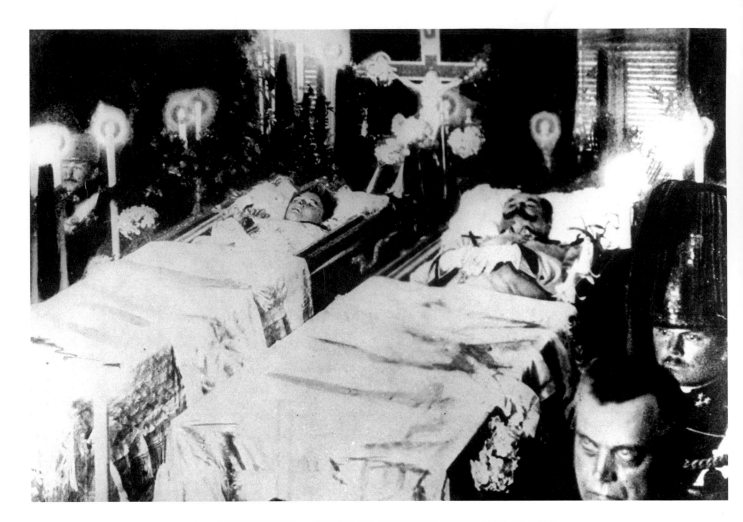

(*clockwise from top*) The bodies of the Archduke and Archduchess lie in state. Members of the Bosnian liberation group attend the trial of the conspirators responsible for the death of Ferdinand and Sophia. The men accused of the murder are brought to court – "1" is Princip, "2" is Danilo Ilitch, and "3" is Cabrinovic. Princip in jail, awaiting trial. Ilitch, seen as the leader of the conspiracy and subsequently hanged by the Austrians.

The first struck the Archduchess in the abdomen. The second hit the Archduke in the neck and pierced his jugular vein. Before losing consciousness, he pleaded "Sophia dear! Don't die! Stay alive for our children!" The car drove off at speed, heading for the Governor's residence. Although both victims were still alive when they got there, they died soon afterwards.

Back at the scene of the crime, Princip had been seized by members of the escort, beaten on the head with the flat of their swords, knocked to the ground and kicked, before being hurried away to spend the rest of his life in prison.

As a direct result of the killings, exactly one month later, Austria declared war on Serbia. The Russian army was mobilized to protect Serbia, and Germany then delivered an ultimatum to Russia. On August 1, Germany declared war on Russia. France mobilized her armies on the same day. Two days later Germany declared war on France and invaded Belgium. As guarantors of Belgian independence, Britain declared war on Germany. Over the next four years, some 15 million men lost their lives in the war that followed, and at the end of it, the Austrian Empire to which poor Franz Ferdinand had been heir, no longer existed.

In August 1940 the attention of much of the world was focused on Europe, where World War II was at last in its full horrific glory. Hitler's Luftwaffe were making their daily raids on England. France had already been conquered, the Netherlands overrun, and the battle for North Africa was under way. The assassination of Leon Trotsky was almost sidelined by such events – a grim killing by Stalinist agents, operating far from home in Mexico City.

The row between Stalin and Trotsky had come to a head in late 1926. Stalin, whose own hold on sanity was often precarious, believed that Trotsky had "gone raving mad". Never one to accept opposition, Stalin began to hound all those he called "October leaders", pre-eminently Trotsky, who had to set up an underground press to print his program for the 1927 Party Congress. On November 7, the last two open demonstrations against Stalin took place. A week later Trotsky and Grigory Zinoviev, another Bolshevik leader, were expelled from the Party. Trotsky was evicted from his apartment in the Kremlin, and was finally exiled from the Soviet Union in January 1929.

There were those who wondered why Stalin had not ordered his killing then and there, but Stalin was a cunning man, who knew that Trotsky would act as a figure round which opposition to the Soviet government would rally. Stalin would thus always know where to find his enemies. Trotsky did not have the same comfort. Wherever he went, he could never be sure that an assassin was not lurking in the shadows.

Finally, on August 21, 1940, the assassin emerged from the shadows, a man named Mercader who had been a frequent visitor to Trotsky's home. The former lieutenant in the Spanish Republican Army split Trotsky's skull with an ice-axe, piercing the brain of which Trotsky had been so proud. At long last, Stalin was the sole survivor of the old Bolshevik triumvirate.

Trotsky Assassination

Scientists in Mexico City begin their examination of Trotsky's brain following his assassination, August 21, 1940.

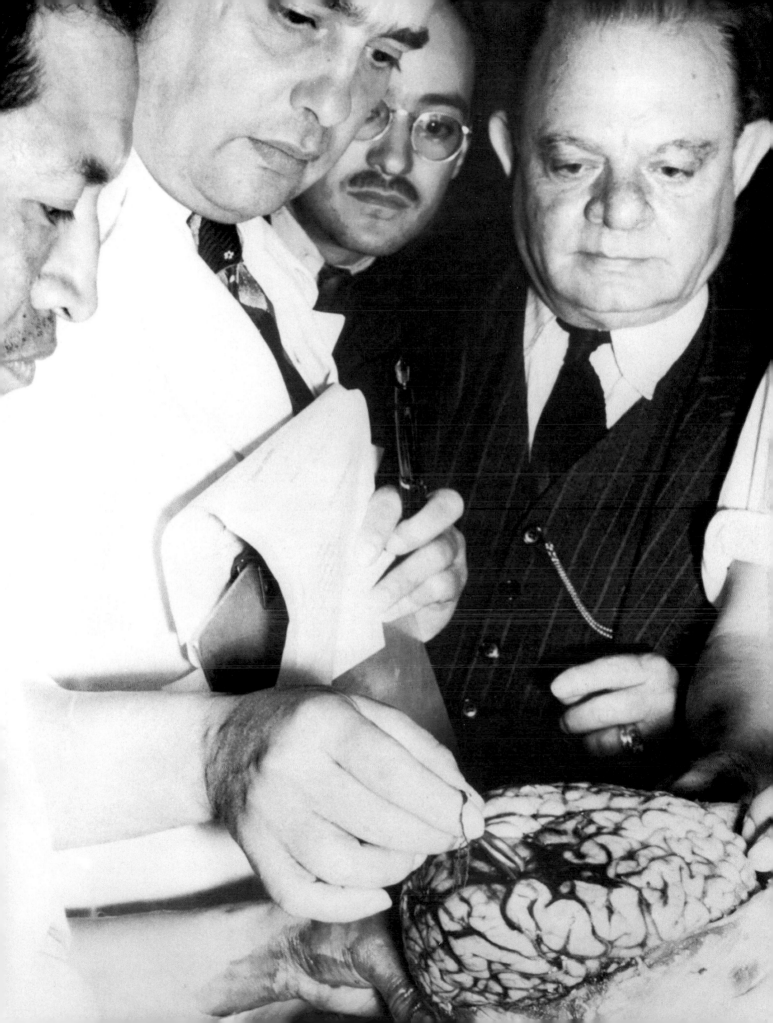

By the summer of 1944 it was clear to many high-ranking officers in the Wehrmacht that Germany was in the hands of a madman. Grinding defeats on both the Western and Eastern Fronts seemed not to have registered with Hitler, whose insane optimism was increasingly based on unworkable strategies and phantom armies. While Hitler fumed and sacked his generals, opposition grew within Army High Command. Under the leadership of General Ludwig Beck and Field Marshal Erwin von Witzleben, a plot was hatched to assassinate the Führer.

On the morning of July 20, 1944 Oberst Claus Schenk, Count von Stauffenberg, entered the "Wolf's Lair" – the name given to Hitler's command headquarters at Rastenburg, on the Prussian Eastern Front. Hitler was about to hold a conference here with other senior members of the General Staff. Stauffenberg, a war-hero and an aristocrat who loathed Hitler, carried a small suitcase which contained a single bomb, one of many British-made bombs taken by the Abwehr, the German intelligence organization. He placed the suitcase under the table at which Hitler would be seated, activated the timer, and left the building in haste, heading for Berlin, where the plotters intended to seize power in a military coup.

The bomb exploded. Others were killed, but Hitler was only slightly injured. The following day he broadcast to the German people, pointing out that his escape was proof that he was to complete his tasks "under the protection of a divine power". Those responsible for the explosion had no such protection. Von Stauffenberg was captured and immediately shot. Other conspirators had the sense to take the offer of taking their own lives as punishment. Those who were least fortunate were hanged from meat-hooks with piano wire, their executions filmed for the enjoyment of Hitler and senior members of the Nazi Party, and as a warning to other army officers.

Hitler Bomb Plot

Claus Schenk, Count von Stauffenberg, the man who led the assassination attempt on Adolf Hitler.

President John F. Kennedy was shot and killed while traveling in a limousine along Elm Street, Dallas on the afternoon of November 22, 1963. Three quarters of an hour after the attack, a man named Lee Harvey Oswald was arrested on a charge of murdering police officer J. D. Tippit. During police interrogation, he was further charged with the assassination of the President. Two days later, while in police custody and on police premises, in front of dozens of reporters and millions watching on live television, Oswald was gunned down and killed by a club owner named Jack Ruby. And that is as much as the world knows for certain about the most famous assassination of the 20th century.

That afternoon, Kennedy's body was flown in Air Force One to Andrews Air Base, and then driven to the Bethesda Naval Hospital in Washington D.C., where the autopsy was performed. Three days later came the funeral – chilling, emotional, reverential, ceremonious. The image of Kennedy's three-year-old son saluting as his father's coffin passed by became an icon of the brief but brilliant Kennedy era.

A week after the killing, Kennedy's successor, President Lyndon Johnson, appointed the Warren Commission to investigate what had happened. Apart from Earl Warren himself, the Commission consisted of six members: one Republican and one Democrat senator, one Democrat and one Republican member of the House of Representatives (the latter being Gerald Ford), a former President of the World Bank, and a former Director of the CIA. Ten months later the Commission issued its report. There had been no conspiracy. Oswald had acted alone, firing three shots from his Mannlicher–Carcano rifle on the sixth floor of the Schoolbook Depository Building. One of these shots had missed the President's limousine altogether. Another had struck Kennedy in the back, passed through his throat and gone on to hit Governor Connally in the back, ending up

JFK Assassination

Robert Kennedy (left), Jacqueline Kennedy, and Edward Kennedy stand at the graveside during the funeral of John F. Kennedy, Arlington, Virginia, November 24, 1963.

embedded in the Governor's thigh. This was later to be dubbed the "magic bullet". The third shot had hit Kennedy in the head. The limousine had then been driven at speed to the Parkland Hospital. The President was virtually dead on arrival.

But, while the Commission was compiling its report, other versions of what happened were beginning to emerge. It was alleged that Kennedy had been killed on the orders of Mafia boss Carlos Marcello; on the orders of Lyndon Johnson; by disgruntled Cuban ex-pats angry at Kennedy's soft-handed approach to Castro; by the CIA; by agents of the Soviet Union; by the "Umbrella Man" and a dark-complexioned accomplice who were caught on camera at the side of Elm Street as the Presidential motorcade swept by.

Once the Warren Report was published, doubt was also cast on its explanation that Ruby's killing of Oswald had

been a spontaneous act – the motive for which was to spare Jackie Kennedy, the President's widow, the pain of a trial. Firearms experts doubted that Oswald was a good enough marksman to score two hits in three shots fired in six to nine seconds from an elevation of some 60 feet at a moving target. The profusion of such doubts, and the airing of conspiracy theories in a succession of books, films, and articles, prompted the appointment in 1976 of a second enquiry – the House Select Committee on Assassinations (HSCA). This second report stated that four shots had been fired (including one from the famous "grassy knoll"), suggested that Ruby had an accomplice in the police who helped him gain access to Oswald, and questioned whether the security arrangements for Kennedy's visit to Dallas had been adequate. The HSCA also noted that in the three years directly following the slaying, 18 material witnesses had died – six by gunfire, three in motor accidents, two by their own hand, one from a cut throat, one from a blow to the

(*opposite*) Bloodstains are visible on the back seat of the convertible in which JFK was shot while riding through Dallas, November 22, 1963. (*above*) New York City commuters read of the tragedy on their way home. (*left*) TV anchorman Walter Cronkite weeps on camera as he announces the President's death, November 22, 1963.

neck, three from heart attacks, and two from other natural causes.

More than 40 years on, the world will never know what really happened. What is astonishing is that, at a time when the population United States was still reeling with shock and grief, it was possible for so many questions to go unanswered, for so many suspect statements to go unchallenged and for the investigation to wither so quickly. The hurry to get back to business as usual was almost unseemly.

(*above*) Vice President Lyndon B. Johnson takes the presidential oath on board Air Force One just a few hours after JFK's assassination. Events were moving very swiftly. (*right*) The American media identify Lee Harvey Oswald and the gun he is carrying as the man and the weapon responsible for Kennedy's death. (*opposite*) Lee Harvey Oswald's body lies on a stretcher moments after he was killed by Jack Ruby, November 24, 1963.

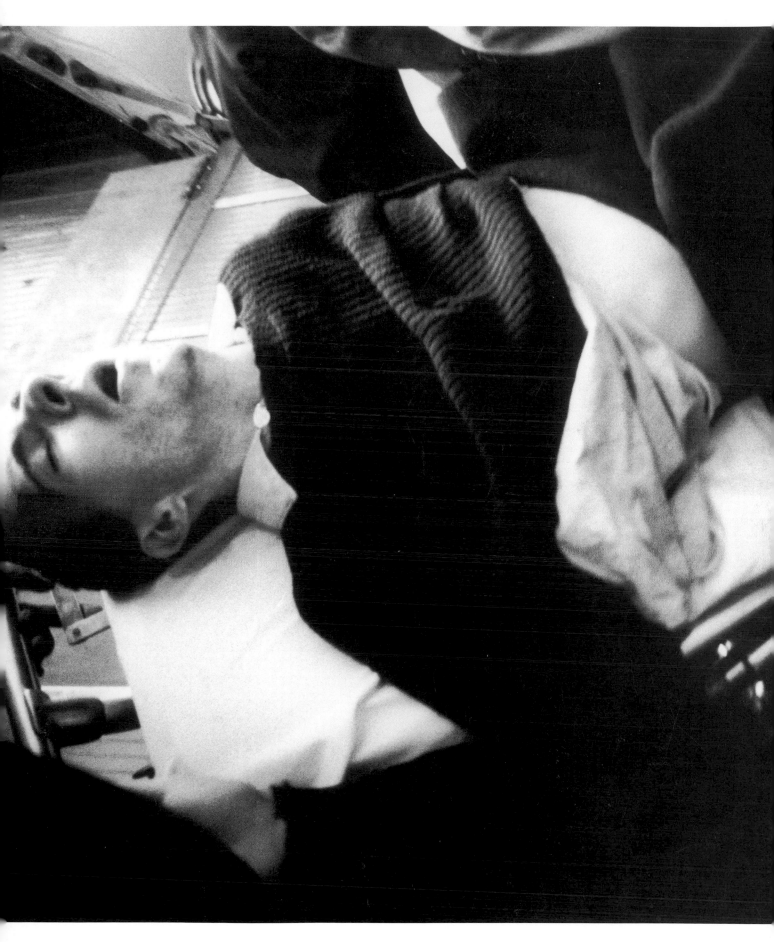

It was the second killing to rock the entire United States within five years. First there was Kennedy in Dallas, then there was the Reverend Martin Luther King Jnr. in Memphis. Two high-powered rifles and a handful of bullets had done their best to wipe out the entire American dream of a new age of life, liberty, and the pursuit of happiness.

By 1968 King, in his late thirties, was a man who had realized a great deal of his own personal dream, but the struggle to achieve justice for the black and white alike went on unabated. In March, with the Southern Christian Leadership Conference, King launched the Poor People's Campaign, on behalf of the low-paid and unemployed. On April 3, King delivered his famous "Mountaintop" speech:

"It really doesn't matter what happens now.... some began to... talk about the threats that were out – what would happen to me from some of our sick white brothers.... Like anybody, I would like to live a long life... but I'm not concerned about that now. I just want to do God's will. And He's allowed me to go up to the mountain. And I've looked over, and I've seen the Promised Land. I may not get there with you. But I want you to know tonight, that we, as a people, will get to the Promised Land. And so I'm happy tonight. I'm not worried about anything. I'm not fearing any man. Mine eyes have seen the glory of the coming of the Lord..."

The following evening, King was shot in the throat as he stood on the balcony of his room at the Lorraine Motel in Memphis, Tennessee. The Reverend Jesse Jackson was with him when it happened: "He had just bent over. I reckon if he had been standing up he would not have been hit in the face." A single shot was fired.

Martin Luther King Assassination

A great man laid low... The body of Martin Luther King Junior, April 8, 1968

Two months later, an escaped convict named James Earl Ray was captured at London's Heathrow Airport. Extradited to Tennessee, Ray subsequently confessed to the killing. But, as in the case of the assassination of JFK, many doubts as to the true killer having been identified remained. Ray had no motive to kill King. He was not a trained marksman. None of Ray's fingerprints were found in the motel room from which the shot was supposed to have come. The bullet that killed King was never matched to Ray's weapon. Witnesses surrounding King at the time of his death said that the shot had come from another location.

The immediate effects of King's death were to make many streets unsafe for white men, to provoke rioting in more than 60 cities, and for a dusk to dawn curfew to be imposed in Memphis itself. The longer term result was for an entire generation to be plunged into a grief from which it never fully recovered.

(*above top*) Civil Rights leader Andrew Young (on left) and other witnesses indicate the position of the assassin, Lorraine Motel, April 4, 1968. (*left*) The blood of Martin Luther King Junior on the motel balcony. (*opposite top*) James Earl Ray takes the oath before the Washington committee, August 1968. (*opposite below*) Coretta Scott King at the funeral of her husband, Martin Luther King Jr, April 9, 1968.

At 12:15 A.M. on June 5, 1968 – shortly after winning the California Primary in his presidential campaign – Senator Robert F. Kennedy left the ballroom of the Ambassador Hotel, Los Angeles, to give a press conference. His route took him through a small pantry, and here he was shot. Three bullets hit him, one in the head and two near his right armpit. Minutes later, by coincidence, all three television networks began coverage.

People in the ballroom heard muffled sounds. Kennedy's brother-in-law, Steven Smith, asked everyone to clear the room. Rumors spread that Kennedy had been shot. News reports said he was conscious and had "good color". Over the next 24 hours Kennedy's Press Secretary Frank Mankiewicz kept the public informed from the Good Samaritan Hospital. Then, early on the morning of June 6, came the news. Kennedy was dead. The young assailant held to be responsible was variously described as being a Filipino, a Mexican, a Jamaican, and a Cuban. Eventually he was identified as Sirhan B. Sirhan, a Palestinian whom eyewitnesses reported had shouted "I did it for my country" shortly after the shooting.

The Curse on the Kennedys had struck again, less than five years after the death of JFK. And, as in the Dallas shooting, there were subsequent allegations of conspiracy. A woman in a polka-dot dress and a young man had been seen running from the hotel just after the shooting, crying out "We shot him!" More bullets had been fired than could have come from Sirhan's gun. Evidence disappeared. LA Police Department photographs of the crime scene were destroyed.

Sirhan at first confessed to the crime, but subsequently claimed he was confused by the repeated hypnosis he was given to extract further information. Under Californian law, he was due for release in 1984, but was still in prison in 2006, having been denied parole 13 times.

Killing of Robert Kennedy

Busboy Juan Romero gently raises the head of the dying Robert Kennedy, June 5, 1968.

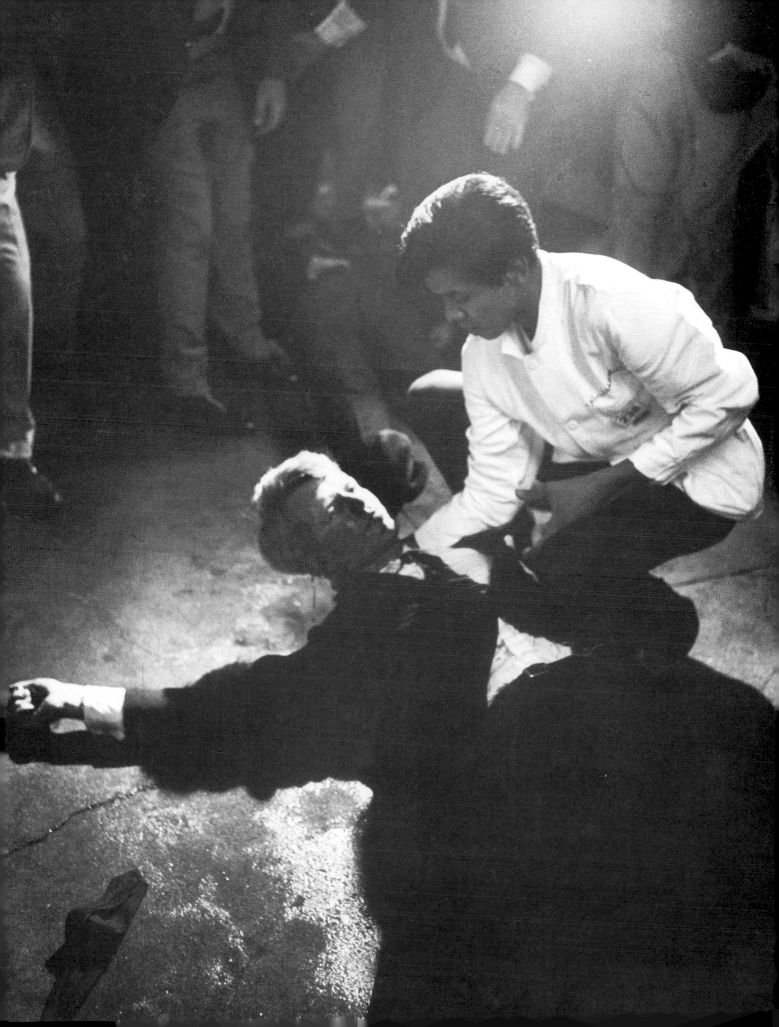

Late in 1980, John Lennon was in New York City, working on a new album. On December 6, Mark David Chapman boarded a plane in Hawaii and took off for New York. What he later described as "a small voice" was telling him to kill the ex-Beatle.

Two days later, at around 5:00 P.M. Lennon and his wife Yoko Ono left their apartment in The Dakota at West 72nd Street to go to the Record Plant Studio. As they did so several people approached asking for their autographs. One of them was Mark Chapman, who had with him a copy of the album *Double Fantasy* and the novel *The Catcher in the Rye* by J. D. Salinger. John and Yoko drove off. Some six hours later they returned. Chapman was waiting for them.

As they walked towards the apartment building, Chapman called out: "Mr. Lennon". He then dropped into what the police called "a combat stance" and fired five shots from a Charter Arms .38 caliber revolver. One shot missed, but two hit Lennon in the left side of his back, and two more in his left shoulder. The bullets had been specially filed to inflict maximum injury. Lennon said "I'm hit", and fell on to the sidewalk. He was rushed by the police to the Roosevelt Hospital where he died, having lost 80 percent of his blood. News of his death was broadcast and a crowd gathered outside The Dakota, burning candles, praying, and singing Lennon's songs.

Chapman never denied his crime. He said that he had felt if he shot Lennon he would "become something", that his motive had been envy of Lennon's wealth and fame, and that a "small voice" had told him him to "Just do it". He was sentenced to serve 20 years to life and has been denied parole three times.

Killing of John Lennon

Two in a vast crowd of mourners following the death of John Lennon, Central Park, New York City, December 1980.

Four U.S. presidents have been assassinated while in office: Lincoln, Garfield, McKinley, and John F. Kennedy. None was killed in the White House or in any of the other presidential abodes. None was killed outside the United States. Only while on public display in their own country have U.S. presidents come to grief.

The last to have suffered a serious attack on his life was Ronald Reagan on March 30, 1981. He was walking to his car from the Washington Hilton Hotel, where he had been addressing a labor convention, when a young man stepped up, confronted the President and fired a series of six shots from a Rohm RG-14 revolver at a distance of 10 feet (3 metres). None of the bullets hit the President directly, but a ricochet pierced his left lung. Ironically, this bullet had bounced off the bullet-proof glass of the presidential car. Three members of the group around Reagan were also hit, most seriously among them his Press Secretary Jim Brady. The assailant was immediately brought to the ground by Secret Service agents. The President was bundled into his car and raced to hospital where he joked with staff in the operating theater, saying "Please tell me you're Republicans" and said to his wife "Honey, I forgot to duck".

The man responsible was a 25-year-old unemployed depressive named John Warnock Hinckley Jnr. During the five years preceding the assassination attempt, Hinckley had become obsessed with the movie *Taxi Driver* and with the movie actress Jodie Foster, to the extent that he had planned to hijack a plane and publicly commit suicide where she could see him. He then formed a plan to assassinate the U.S. President and thus gain sufficient fame to match hers. Hinckley was not particular as to which president he killed, and prior to the attempt on Reagan's life had spent years stalking his predecessor in office, Jimmy Carter.

Reagan Assassination Attempt

John Hinckley Jnr. is driven from the scene of his attempted assassination of President Ronald Reagan, March 30, 1981.

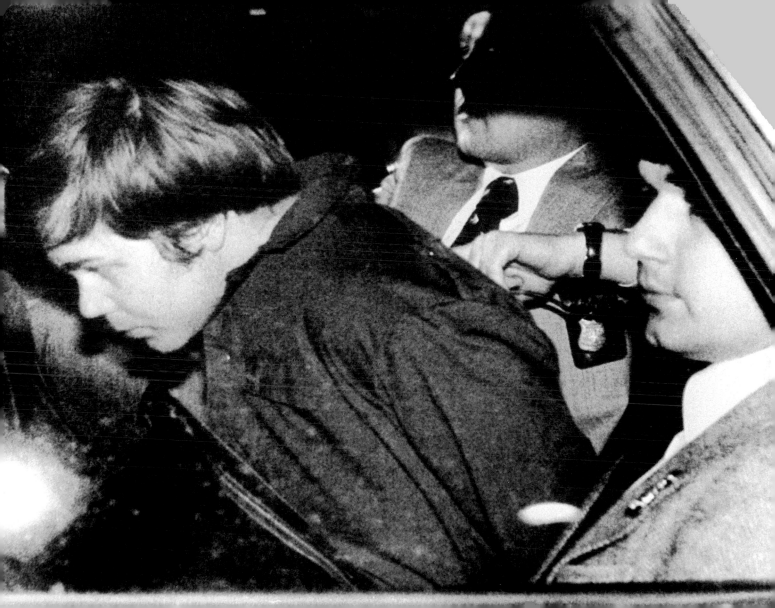

At his trial on June 21, 1982, Hinckley was found "not guilty" by reason of insanity, although the prosecution had insisted that he was legally sane. The verdict incensed many Americans and four states abolished the insanity defense as a result. Hinckley was confined at St. Elizabeth's Hospital in Washington D.C. After 17 years he was allowed to leave the hospital for limited and supervised visits to his parents. A year later these visits became longer and it was felt that supervision was not required, but the privilege was revoked when it was discovered that Hinckley had smuggled materials about Foster back into the hospital. He remains under close supervision.

The assassination attempt on Ronald Reagan. (*top*) In light rain, Reagan waves to crowds as he leaves the Hilton Hotel. (*above*) Police and Secret Service agents dive to protect the President and overpower Hinckley. (*opposite*) The worst is over, but three victims lie on the sidewalk: Press Secretary James Brady, Agent Timothy McCarthy, and Officer Thomas Delahanty.

The Act of Murder

A man lies in a pool of his own blood. Photographed by
Weegee on January 1, 1939, the victim had been shot
dead after an argument over a game of bowls.

On the night of September 14, 1922, the Reverend Edward Hall, rector of St. John's Episcopal Church in the New Jersey town of New Brunswick, arranged to meet Mrs Eleanor Mills, wife of the church's sexton. It turned out to be their last meeting. Thirty-six hours later their bodies were found by another courting couple in the shade of a roadside crab-apple tree.

The affair between rector and sexton's wife was known to others, among them – so the police believed – the rector's wife Frances Hall and her two brothers, Henry and William Stevens. Four years later, Widow Hall and the Stevens boys were brought to trial for the double murder. The motive was convincing enough, but the evidence was extremely weak. Henry Carpender, Frances Hall's cousin was charged with complicity in the murders.

Louise Geist, a former parlor-maid to the Halls, was also called, but then said that she had no evidence to give. Jane Gibson, known in the community as "the Pig Woman", was a neighbor of the Halls. She claimed she had overheard an argument between them, that she had witnessed a struggle, and that this had been followed by a scream and four gunshots. She gave her evidence dramatically, for she suffered from a kidney complaint and addressed the court from a stretcher, while her own mother sat beside her shouting "She's a liar! That's what she's always been!" It was said that the Pig Woman had made up her story for the sake of publicity. For her own part, Frances Hall claimed that at the time of the murders she and her brother William had been in church.

The trial lasted a month, all four accused were acquitted, and since that time no one has admitted to the killings and no names have been put forward as possible killers. The best guess would seem to be that the Reverend Hall and Mrs. Mills were murdered by the KKK, as punishment for their sin of adultery.

Crab-Apple Tree Murders

The "Pig Woman" testifies from her cot in court during the Crab-Apple Tree Murder Trial at Somerville, New Jersey in 1922.

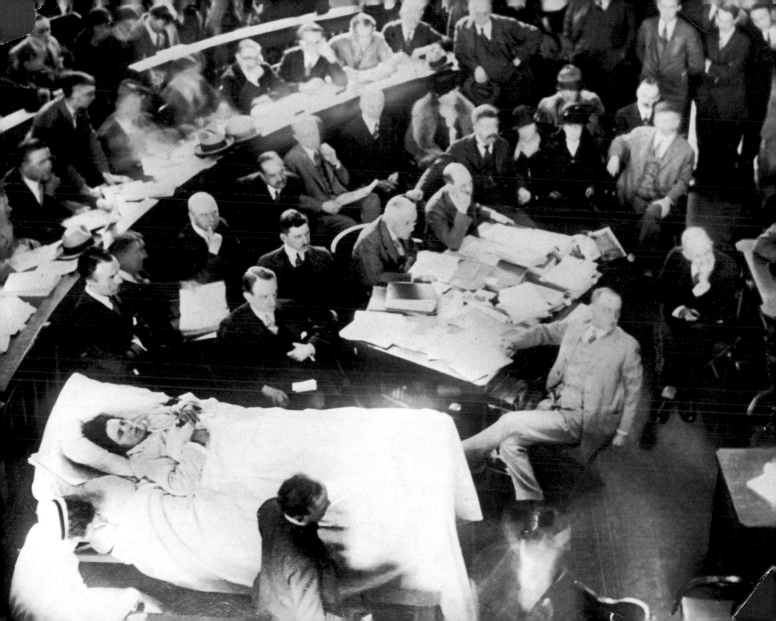

James Riddle "Jimmy" Hoffa was born on St. Valentine's Day 1913. His rise to fame and power was swift. The son of a poor coal miner, Hoffa helped organize his first strike as a teenager, and was still in his 20s when he was elected President of the Michigan Conference of Teamsters. In 1957 he took over the National Presidency of the Teamsters.

Hoffa liked power and those who wielded it – if they were on his side. He was on friendly terms with the Mob, J. Edgar Hoover and Richard Nixon, but loathed the Kennedys – Robert Kennedy believed that Hoffa had pocketed some $9.5 million of Union funds. Some say that Hoffa was deeply involved in a conspiracy to kill JFK, and that in July 1963 Hoffa met with Mob leaders Santos Trafficante and Carlos Marcello in a New Orleans hotel to plan the hit. Marcello is reported as telling Frank Ragano, a Mob lawyer, after JFK's death: "When you see Jimmy Hoffa, you tell him he owes me, and he owes me big".

In 1967 Hoffa was sentenced to 15 years for attempted bribery of a grand juror, but was released in 1971 when Nixon commuted the sentence on condition that Hoffa gave up union work for the next 10 years. Then, at 2:30 P.M. on July 30, 1975 Hoffa disappeared from the parking lot of a restaurant in a suburb of Detroit. He had been due to meet two Mafia leaders, Tony Jack Giacolone and Tony "Pro" Provenzano. His body has never been found.

There have been many theories as to what happened: that he was dumped in Lake Erie; under the New Jersey Turnpike; beneath the turf of the Giants Stadium; in an abandoned coal mine; in a landfill on Staten Island; that his body lies in Presley's grave, that it was put through a wood chipper and fed to hogs, that it was mixed with concrete and used in construction, dissolved in acid and used to re-chrome car bumpers. The search continues.

Jimmy Hoffa

Teamsters leader James R. Hoffa peers at his reflection, April 11, 1959. He was then approaching the height of his power.

It took over half an hour to kill Kitty Genovese. Early on the morning of March 13, 1964 she drove home from her job as bar manager at Ev's Eleventh Hour Club in Queen's to her apartment in Kew Gardens. She parked her car and locked it. She had then only some 30 feet to walk to the door of the apartment block, but there was someone waiting for her. The man caught up with her near the street light at the end of the parking lot. He stabbed her several times. She screamed. Several people heard her. One man opened his window and shouted down to the attacker, "Hey, leave that girl alone!" The attacker moved off.

Kitty, bleeding profusely, managed to stagger to the side wall of the apartment block. Moving at all was painful and difficult. In all probability she was dying. Minutes passed. The attacker returned and stabbed her again. "I'm dying," she cried. Again the attacker fled, this time to his white Chevy. To those watching from other apartments, it appeared that he drove away.

Kitty now stumbled to the rear of the apartment block. She reached the hallway and slumped to the floor. The attacker had not driven away, and he now followed the trail of blood until he found her. He stripped her dying body and sexually assaulted her. He later told the police: "I came back because I knew I'd not finished what I set out to do". He took $49 from her wallet, stabbed her yet again, got back into his car and finally drove away.

Some 37 people saw what was happening and did nothing about, neither seeking to intervene nor calling the police. It was this failure on the part of the public that made the killing big news, and six days later Winston Moseley, a machine operator with no previous convictions, was arrested and charged with the murder of Kitty Genovese. He was found guilty of murder in the first degree.

Winston Moseley

The doorway in which Kitty Genovese was repeatedly stabbed by Winston Moseley on the night of March 13, 1964.

Teenager Robert Chambers had been in trouble much of his life. He was raised in New York City, where he had been to a succession of smart prep schools, at all of which he obtained poor grades and exhibited bad behavior in the form of stealing and drug abuse. On leaving school and moving to Boston University, the behavior worsened. Chambers was now committing petty theft and burglary, and had both drug and alcohol dependency problems.

Early on the morning of August 26, 1986 Chambers had a row with his girlfriend in a bar on the Upper East Side. He then left the bar with another young woman, Jennifer Levin. Later that day Levin's semi-clad body was found beneath an elm tree close to the Metropolitan Museum of Art. Chambers himself watched as police officers investigated the crime scene. There were scratches on his face and arms.

Patrons at the bar where Levin had last been seen identified Chambers as the young man with whom she had left on the night of the killing. When police interviewed Chambers he changed his story several times, but ended by saying that Levin had tied his hands with her panties and then sexually assaulted him. He had been able to break free, and that was when she had been killed. The Assistant District Attorney was unimpressed by this story.

When Chambers came to trial, the newspapers called the crime "The Preppy Murder". At first there were signs that maybe they were on the side of Chambers. Levin's character was attacked. She was labelled a "teenage vamp", while Chambers was the "ex-altar boy". The defense at Chambers's trial referred to a "sex diary" that Levin kept. There was no such diary.

The Preppy Killer was charged with manslaughter in the first degree. He was released from prison on St. Valentine's Day 2003.

Preppy Killer

Robert Chambers wears a confident, almost truculent air as he strides through New York City on March 22, 1988.

The death of seven-year-old Megan Kanka in 1994 had repercussions around the world and led to a fundamental change in U.S. law. The stories of both Megan's death and the life of her killer tell of violence and abuse on an horrendous scale, and of how the harm that is done to a child can come back to haunt society a generation later.

Megan's killer was 33-year-old Jesse Timmendequas, a man who had lived through childhood horror. Jesse's father – Charles Hall – had been released from prison when Jesse was seven, and had then begun a rule of violence and brutality in the family home. Hall repeatedly beat and raped Jesse and his younger brother, drowned their dog in front of them and cut the head off the family cat. When the adult Jesse was charged with the death of Megan, Hall said he hoped that his son would go to the chair. Jesse Timmedequas had been in serious trouble before his dreadful attack on Megan. In 1979 he pleaded guilty to attempted aggravated sexual assault of a five-year-old in New Jersey. Two years later, he was sentenced to six years in prison for sexually assaulting another seven-year-old. The attack on Megan came 12 years later.

Jesse lived just across the street from Megan. One day, offering to show her a puppy, he lured her into his house, raped her, killed her, and then drove her body to a nearby country park. The following day he led police to her body. He was charged with murder and sentenced to death.

Shock waves from the crime carried far beyond New Jersey. A campaign rapidly grew seeking to protect communities from men like Jesse Timmendequas, and stating that parents had a right to know when such men lived nearby. After passing through the state legislature, Megan's Law, as it has come to be called, now applies across the United States. The existence of known paedophiles in any neighborhood must now become public knowledge.

Megan's Law

Maureen Kanka, Megan's mother, smiles down at her son Jeremy as they meet President Bill Clinton at the White House, May 17, 1996.

Rock Creek Park runs down through some of Washington D.C.'s more affluent north-west suburbs. It's popular with cyclists and joggers, a pleasant place to picnic, but it has also seen its share of violence over the years. On May 22, 2002, a man walking his dog and looking for turtles in a remote part of the Park found a human skeleton. A police search through dental records revealed that the skeleton was that of 24-year-old Chandra Levy, who had just finished an internship at the Federal Bureau of Prisons. She had been missing for just over a year. Further examination suggested that she had been murdered.

At the time of her disappearance, Chandra had been due to fly home to Modesto, California. She was last seen leaving a Health Club, and her bag was already packed. From the moment she disappeared, Chandra was headline news, for there were strong rumors that she had been having an affair with Republican Congressman Gary Condit. Condit refused to confirm or deny the affair, but the rumors alone were enough to cost him his seat in Congress when he came up for re-election.

Rumors spread. Parallels were drawn between the Condit–Levy affair and that of Clinton and Monica Lewinsky. Speculation grew, becoming wilder and wilder. It was suggested that Levy had been working for the Israeli Secret Service Mossad, seeking inside military and defense information. An unlikely link was drawn between Chandra Levy's death and the execution of Timothy McVeigh, the Oklahoma Bomber. More credible was a link between her death and that of Joyce Chiang, a young attorney who had worked for the Immigration and Naturalization Service, and whose body had been discovered in a D.C. federal park two years earlier.

As of February 2000, the killing of Chandra Levy has been listed as a "cold case" by the Washington D.C. Police department. The FBI investigation remains open.

Chandra Levy

Washington D.C. police photos of the missing Chandra Levy. The different wigs were an attempt to help identify her should she have changed her hair style.

It took the police over three months to find Laci Peterson's body. She had disappeared from the Modesto home that she shared with her husband Scott on Christmas Eve, 2002. Her family saw this as an odd time for Laci to choose to make an unscheduled trip, the more so since she was seven-and-a-half months pregnant.

Family and friends had been right to worry, for on April 13, 2003 the body of a male child, with his umbilical cord still attached, was found on the shore of San Francisco Bay, north of Berkeley, California. The following day all that remained of Laci Peterson was recovered a mile along the shore. As a result of decomposition her body was without head, arms, and legs, and so DNA testing was the only means of identifying both mother and child.

Suspicion did not fall immediately on Scott Peterson. He had showed concern for his wife and had been co-ordinating the volunteers who had been searching for Laci. But two weeks after her disappearance Modesto police obtained photographs of Scott posing with another woman. By the time Laci's body was found, they already suspected he was responsible for her death. When they arrested him, he was driving a car he had bought by falsely using his mother's name, and carrying $15,000 in cash. He had dyed his hair blonde.

His trial for the murder of Laci and Conner (the name that had been chosen for the baby) ended on November 12, 2004. Scott Peterson was found guilty of murder in the first degree in the case of Laci and of murder in the second degree in the case of Conner. He was sentenced to death by lethal injection. The case led to the United States Congress passing the Unborn Violence Act, more popularly known as Laci and Conner's Law. It came into force on April 1, 2004, its purpose being to establish that a "child in utero" shall be considered a separate human being where a pregnant woman is subjected to any form of violence.

Scott Peterson

Scott Peterson, during a hearing at the Stanislaus Superior Court In Modesto, California on May 2, 2003.

Crimes of Passion

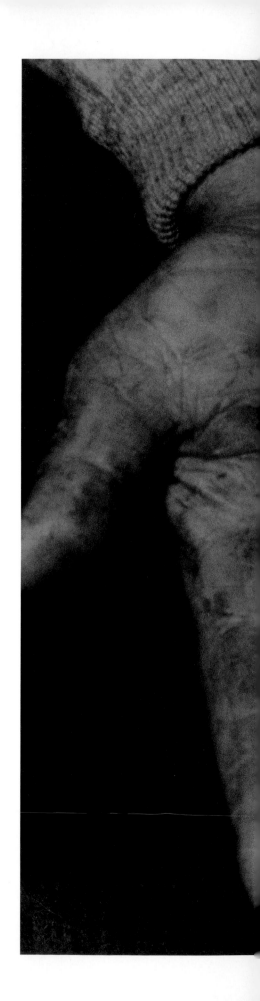

A police shot of the blood-stained hands of Zein Isa on November 7, 1989. Isa, a Palestinian emigré living in St. Louis, had stabbed and murdered his daughter, Tina, after she rebelled against his orders.

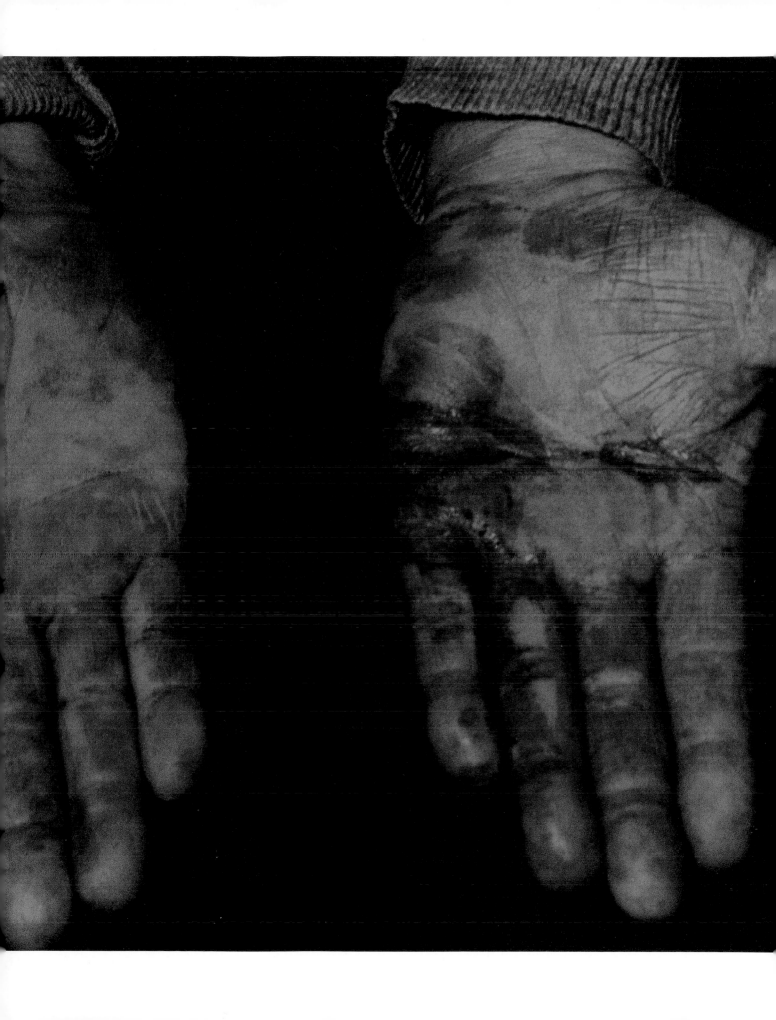

On a hot summer's night in June 1906, New York City's wealthy elite gathered on the roof of Madison Square Garden for the opening night of *Mamzelle Champagne*. Alone at a table near the stage sat Stanford White, the architect of the building and a man who had "ruined" many a young woman. White was a married man, but it was known that he kept a bachelor apartment for this express purpose, and among those he had lured there was Evelyn Nesbit, a very young and very beautiful showgirl.

The relationship between White and Nesbit, which had begun when White slipped something into Nesbit's champagne, ended when she married Henry "Harry" Kendall Thaw, a multi-millionaire heir to an iron and railroad fortune. Thaw was a jealous and cruel man, with a reputation for taking the whip to any man, woman, or animal who annoyed him. Poor Evelyn had annoyed him on their honeymoon night. Stanford White permanently enraged him, and Thaw had come to Madison Square Garden that June night to execute justice on the man who had so evilly seduced his wife four years earlier.

The band and chorus were in the middle of a number called *I Could Have Loved A Million Girls* when Thaw walked up to White's table. Only the hat-check girl seemed to have thought it strange that Thaw was wearing an overcoat on such a hot night. Thaw took a revolver from the pocket of the coat and fired three times into White's face from point-blank range. At first, the audience thought this was part of the show, but screams broke out when they saw White's mangled and bloody face.

Thaw spent the next nine months in prison, awaiting trial and feeding off meals sent in daily from Delmonico's. He was found not guilty of murder by reason of insanity, and was committed to an asylum. A couple of years later he escaped, fled to Canada, and was recaptured. He was finally declared sane and released in 1915. One of his first acts as a free man was to divorce Evelyn.

Stanford White Killing

Evelyn Nesbit, later Mrs. Harry Thaw, whose beauty lay behind the killing of Stanford White.

Harry Houdini was the most famous magician and escapologist of all time. He was born in Budapest, Hungary, in 1874, although he claimed to have been born in Wisconsin. He began his professional career in 1891, doing card tricks, but was soon experimenting with escape acts. By 1904 he was a sensation, a man who could escape from handcuffs, chains, and straitjackets – often while suspended on a rope or immersed in water. His most famous act was the "Chinese Water Torture", in which he had to escape from a glass and steel cabinet full of water, in which he had been placed upside-down. Houdini could hold his breath for three minutes, essential to this trick, while the audience gasped with terror.

His last performance was at the Garrick Theater in Detroit, Michigan on October 24, 1926. An air of mystery hangs about the cause of his death one week later. Officially, he died of peritonitis. Certainly Houdini had been complaining of pains in his stomach earlier in the tour. But it is also said that just before his last performance, he was visited in his dressing room by three students from McGill University, one of whom, J. Gordon Whitehead, asked if it was true that Houdini could withstand any blow to the stomach. Houdini replied that he could. Whitehead then punched him several times in the stomach, although it was clear that Houdini was in pain. One of the other students later gave evidence that Houdini had said that he had not had sufficient time to tense his muscles. Later that night, Houdini collapsed on stage and was rushed to the Grace Hospital, where he died.

This urban legend regarding his death was later embellished, to include the possibility that Whitehead and Houdini had been having a homosexual affair, and that Whitehead intended to kill or at least harm Houdini. Although Houdini's wife claimed that Harry appeared at a series of séances following his death, his spirit had nothing to say on this matter.

Harry Houdini

Ehrich Weiss, better known as Harry Houdini is strapped into a leather jacket to perform one of his many feats of escapology, 1915.

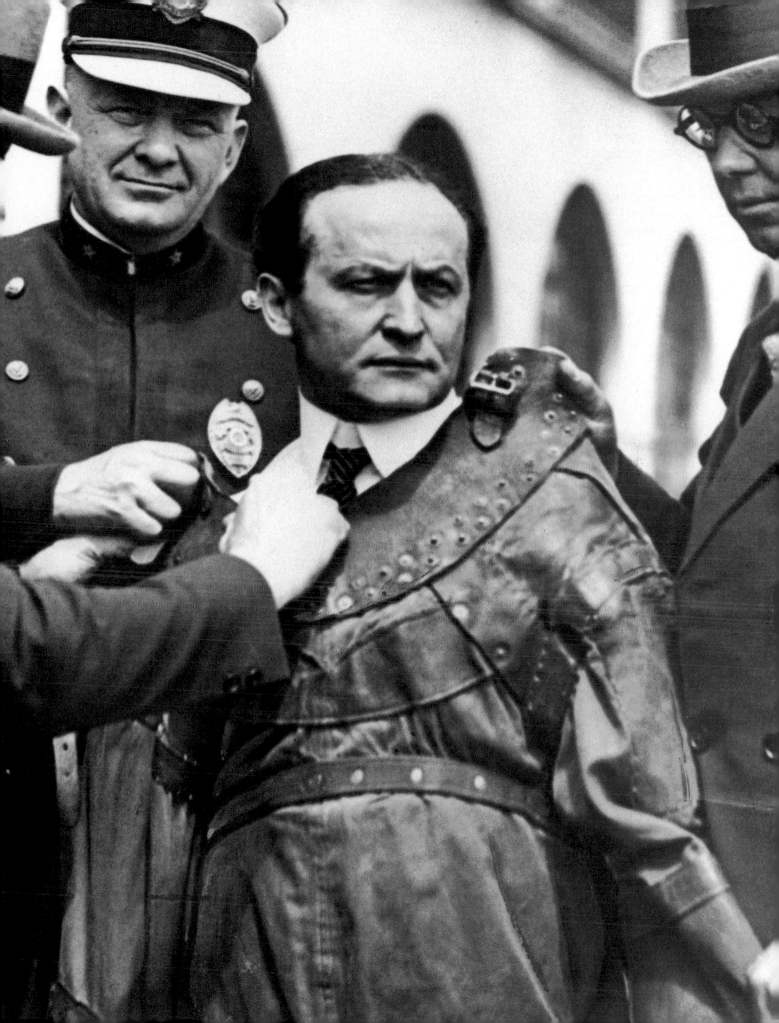

On January 15, 1947 the naked body of a young ex-waitress and aspiring actress named Elizabeth Short was discovered on a vacant lot at 3800 Norton, Leimert Park, Los Angeles. The body had been cut in half and the letters "BD" had been carved on one of the thighs. When news of the discovery was published, the LA Police were inundated with more false confessions to the crime than any other killing has provoked, before or since. Today, criminologists, ex-policemen, and detectives are still arguing as to who killed Elizabeth Short.

The case became known as the Black Dahlia murder, and newspaper reports stated that Short had been given the name "Black Dahlia" while working at a Long Beach drugstore in the summer of 1946 – the year that a movie starring Alan Ladd and Veronica Lake, *The Blue Dahlia,* was released. The police claimed that this story was pure invention on the part of the press, as were reports that Short had been working as a prostitute. What hampered their investigation was that the last verifiable sighting of Short had been at the Biltmore Hotel, almost a week before the discovery of her body.

Among those who confessed to the murder, or have been suspected of it, are: Dr. Walter Alonzo Bayley, a prominent LA surgeon whose daughter was a friend of Short's sister; Norman Chandler, then publisher of the *Los Angeles Times*; Joseph Dumais, a soldier whose confession was subsequently invalidated when it became known that he had been at Fort Dix at the time of the murder; the folk-singer Woody Guthrie; Dr. George Hodel, a mental patient who claimed he was having an affair with Short; and Orson Welles.

The list of suspects, the setting for the killing, and the mystery surrounding the initials "BD" are all worthy of one of Raymond Chandler's crime novels, but the truth as to what happened to Elizabeth Short will almost certainly never now be revealed.

Black Dahlia

Elizabeth Short, aspiring actress and victim in the Black Dahlia mystery killing of 1947.

When Bugsy Siegel was gunned down in June 1947, his West Coast operations were taken over by Mickey Cohen. Cohen lacked Siegels' looks and charm, but still managed to muscle his way into the world of the Hollywood elite. To protect himself and his interests, Cohen hired as his bodyguard an ex-Marine war veteran and gigolo named Johnny Stompanato. One of the many women on whom Stompanato set his sights was the blonde movie star and pin-up Lana Turner. In 1957 he began telephoning her and sending her flowers every day, charming his ways into her favors. Turner wrote later, "His wooing was gentle, persistent and persuasive." Stompanato didn't stop with the mother. He also showered gifts on Turner's daughter, Cheryl Crane. And so the cast was assembled and the stage set for a real-life Hollywood drama.

Turner and Stompanato began living together, and he immediately showed his violent nature, terrifying Turner into compliance with whatever he wanted. The couple stayed together, to the bitter end, which came just after the presentation of the Academy Awards in 1958. Turner had been nominated as Best Actress for her part in *Peyton Place* but lost out to Joanne Woodward. Stompanato watched the ceremony on TV and, when Turner returned home berated her and starting slapping her. "You'll never leave me out of anything like that again," he shouted. Fighting broke out between the two of them spasmodically over the next few days.

On the night of the killing, Cheryl heard Stompanato and her mother rowing. She called out, begging them to stop. Turner ordered her away. Cheryl then heard Stompanato threatening to cut Turner's face and kill her daughter. Cheryl went down to the kitchen, grabbed a carving knife, and returned to her mother's room. This time her mother opened the door. As Cheryl entered the room, Stompanato turned to leave. Knife in hand, Cheryl thrust out her arm. The knife entered Stomapato's stomach and he fell to the floor. Turner hurried her daughter away, phoned for a doctor, and tried to give Stompanato mouth-to-mouth resuscitation. The doctor arrived and

Mickey Cohen and Johnny Stompanato

Mickey Cohen poses to publicize his life story, 1950.

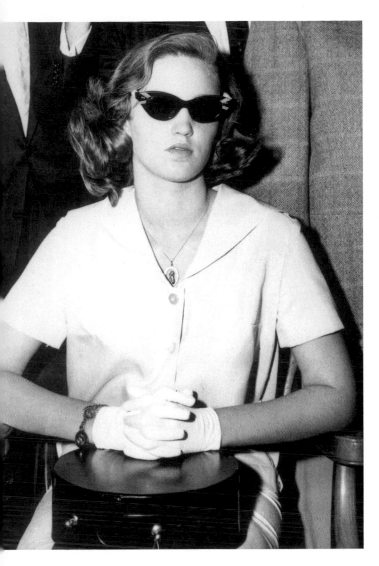

gave Stompanato a shot of adrenaline directly into his heart, but it was too late. The next day crime scene photos of the killing were on the front page of newspapers across the States.

The next step was to "get Geisler". Jerry Geisler was the Hollywood criminal defense attorney. He took the case and drove Turner and Cheryl to the Beverly Hills Police Station. Mickey Cohen now entered to play his part – he had leaked the story to the press. Turner was rich, and Cohen determined to blackmail her. There were some photographs of Turner and Stompanato in circulation which could be used to that effect. "I don't like this thing," he told the press. "There's a lot of unanswered questions… I'm going to find out what happened."

A coroner's inquest was called at the behest of the LA County District Attorney, William B. McKesson, to determine what crime, if any, had been committed. Geisler managed to get Cheryl excused from testifying, on the grounds that she had suffered such trauma. Cohen's testimony was supposedly to identify the victim, but he refused "on the grounds that I may be accused of this murder". That left only Lana Turner to take the stand.

The courtroom was crowded with reporters, microphones, and cameras. Turner entered, dressed in a grey suit, white gloves and stylish hat. Her blonde hair and make-up were impeccable. Her eyes were crystal clear blue. Her manner was faultless. For an hour she answered questions put to her by the coroner and Geisler, breaking down twice, and recovering beautifully. When she left the courtroom, she took the drama with her. The jury took less than half an hour to decide that Stompanato's death was justifiable homicide. McKesson decided no one would be charged. Mickey Cohen was outraged. "So far as that jury's concerned, Johnny just walked too close to that knife."

And so the cast went their separate ways: Turner to a rejuvenated career in TV; Cheryl to live with her grandmother; Cohen to federal prison for income tax violations; and Stompanato to the grave.

(*opposite above*) Johnny Stompanato and Mickey Cohen flank business manager Mike Howard, Los Angeles, 1949. (*opposite below*) Reporters and photographers surround Lana Turner at the trial of her daughter Cheryl Crane. (*above*) Cheryl Crane at the time of her trial for the murder of Stompanato, 1958.

In the summer of 1963, the British establishment was rocked by a scandal of classic proportions, involving call-girls, a Soviet agent, a high-ranking cabinet minister and a society osteopath. Moreover, the settings for this scandal included West End clubs and Cliveden, the Buckinghamshire mansion owned by Lord Astor. The call-girls were Christine Keeler and Mandy Rice-Davies, the agent was Soviet naval attaché Yevgeny Ivanov and the osteopath was Stephen Ward. Ward was a sad character – a man who courted the high life and sought the company of famous people. In so doing he became involved in organizing high-class prostitution. It was Ward who had introduced both Ivanov and the Tory cabinet minister to Keeler. Subsequently, Ward was put on trial for living off "immoral earnings". On the last day of his trial he committed suicide.

The greater shame and the most glaring publicity was reserved, however, for the minister. John Profumo was a Conservative MP and Secretary of State for War in Harold Macmillan's government. Early in 1963, he assured the House of Commons that there had been no impropriety in his relationship with Keeler. Ten weeks later, he admitted to the House that this had been a lie, and once he admitted sleeping with Keeler. It was not long before suggestions were made that he may well have leaked defense secrets to Keeler and that she might have passed them on to Ivanov. Lying to the House was considered an unforgivable trespass. Profumo was forced to resign and a few months later, partly as a result of the fall-out from this scandal, Macmillan and the Conservatives were defeated in the General Election by Harold Wilson and the Labour Party.

In its own way, the Profumo Affair marked the beginning of the Swinging Sixties in Britain – a time when ancient standards and old rules were called into question, and when the British Establishment lost its hitherto engrained and automatic respect. The traditional "elders" and "betters" had been shown in a tawdry and unflattering light, and the press made much of the

Profumo Affair

27 years after the cause célèbre, Christine Keeler recreates her most famous portrait from the Profumo Scandal of 1963.

almost flagrant honesty of both Christine Keeler and Mandy Rice-Davies, who brought a breath of robustly fresh air to the court proceedings.

Quite how far Ward's circle of acquaintances spread was never revealed, but in her 2001 autobiography *The Truth At Last*, Keeler alleged that Ward was indeed running a spy ring for the Soviets. She alleged that his agents included Sir Roger Hollis, then Head of MI5, and Sir Anthony Blunt, surveyor of the Queen's pictures.

Three of the key players in the affair: (*above, left*) Mandy Rice-Davies arrives at court, enjoying every moment of her time in the limelight; (*above*) Stephen Ward, the sinister osteopath at the centre of the affair; and (*left*) Christine Keeler – model, showgirl, call-girl, and innocent destroyer of political careers. (*right*) John Profumo, Conservative MP and War Minister in Harold Macmillan's government.

Amy Fisher was 16 years old when she took her car to an auto shop and met Joey Buttafuoco. He was 35, married with two children. For Amy, it was love at first sight, a love that was consummated in various motel rooms over the next three months. By August 1991, however, Amy was out of school, out of work, and in need of money. Buttafuoco suggested she sign up with a local escort service. Within a month she was making good money as a prostitute.

Her love for Buttafuoco intensified, and she became obsessively jealous of his wife, Mary Jo. She told Buttafuoco that he had to choose between her or his wife, and to her surprise and bitter disappointment, he chose his wife. In her despair Amy made a weak attempt at suicide. She began dating another man, but within a few months resumed her relationship with Joey. What she did not tell him was that she was now planning how to get rid of Mary Jo.

In May 1992 she was ready. A male friend supplied her with a Titan .25 semi-automatic gun and gave her tips on how to use it. On May 17, she and her friend drove to the Buttafuoco home where Amy confronted Mary Jo on her front porch. There was a row, Amy knocked Mary Jo to the ground with the gun, and then shot her in the head. Amy fled. Neighbors rushed to help Mary Jo, and after several hours in surgery Mary Jo's condition stabilized. Four days later police arrested Amy.

The press made the most of the story, dubbing Amy the "Long Island Lolita". Her character was put through the mill. Bail was set at $2 million, and secured only when she agreed to give up the rights to her life story to a production company. After plea bargaining she was sentenced to serve 15 years, and was released in 1999. Buttafuoco was given six months for statutory rape.

Long Island Lolita

Joey Buttafuoco on the steps of his house, September 1992. Though he played a major part in the tragedy, he served only six months in jail.

On July 15, 1997 Gianni Versace, founder of one of the most famous and successful fashion houses in the world, was gunned down, execution-style, by a young man dressed in slacks, a white shirt, a white cap, and wearing a backpack. It was early morning, and Versace was leaving his Miami Beach mansion to make his way to the beach. He was wearing sandals, a dark colored shirt, and shorts with $1,200 in the pocket. None of the money was stolen. Police quickly identified 27-year-old Andrew Cunanan as the sole person responsible for the homicide, although they were hesitant to reveal what motive lay behind the crime.

Later, police announced that Cunanan was suspected of five other murders, which gave a Versace family spokesman the opportunity to state that Versace had been the victim of a maniacal serial killer, and that the motive for the murder was simply madness. Others disagreed, for Cunanan was known to be homosexual and there was evidence that he had met Versace seven years earlier at a costume show in San Francisco, when Versace had approached the young man and said: "I recognize you; where have we known each other from?" There may well have been a mutual attraction. There seems little doubt that Cunanan had become obsessed with Versace, and had been stalking him for five weeks prior to the killing. Some commentators have pointed to the fact that the beach toward which Versace was heading was a meeting place for gays, in-line skaters and, in the words of *Time* magazine, "muscle guys with deltoids like the gas tanks on a Harley".

One week later, Cunanan committed suicide on a houseboat some two miles from the Versace mansion, the scene of the killing. The houseboat mysteriously sank not long after, conveniently destroying any evidence that may have existed on it as to what the real connection was between the fashion billionaire and the backpacker.

Versace Killing

Killer and victim on the cover of *Time* magazine, July 28, 1997. The inset image is of Andrew Cunanan.

JULY 28, 1997 $2.95

TIME

In the Path of A Killer

Gianni Versace
and alleged
serial murderer
Andrew Cunanan

30>

10090

0 724404 1

Kidnappings

Patty Hearst (second from right) is led away from 1827
Golden Gate, San Francisco, by a U.S. Marshall shortly
after her release from captivity on February 16, 1976.

Nathan Leopold and Robert Loeb were exceptionally bright boys. Leopold had an IQ of 220 (genius level), Loeb one of 160. Leopold graduated from the University of Chicago at the age of 18, Loeb from the University of Michigan at 17. But there were flaws in the minds of both of them. For Leopold, it was his passionate belief in Friedrich Nietzsche's concept of the "superman" – someone with an intelligence that placed him justifiably above the laws of society. For Loeb it was an equally passionate belief in the concept of the "perfect crime". In those two beliefs, they were made for each other.

For months they planned, and then on May 21, 1924, they tried their hand at murder. They kidnapped a wealthy young man named Bobby Franks, killed him, and hid his body in a railroad culvert in a suburb of Chicago. There was no motive for the murder save the satisfaction of their vanity. To his great chagrin, however, Leopold learnt that he had left evidence of his involvement with Franks near the poor man's body. Police arrested Leopold and Loeb and they were placed on trial for murder.

They were represented by the most famous criminal defense lawyer of the time, Clarence Darrow. Darrow was growing old and tired, but had already saved more than a hundred criminals from the death penalty, and that was the best Leopold and Loeb could hope for. He told them to plead "not guilty by reason of insanity", a totally new plea, and then fought for them solely on the issue of the sentence they would receive. He based his defense on three issues: 1. that Leopold and Loeb did not believe that what they had done was wrong and were therefore not responsible for their actions; 2. that the state of Illinois had never executed anyone below the age of 23; and 3. that execution was not a "logical punishment for the crime".

Darrow had his way, and the two brilliant young men were sentenced to life imprisonment.

Leopold and Loeb

Nathan Leopold (right) and Richard Loeb, perpetrators of the "perfect crime" come face to face in police custody.

In 1927 Charles A. Lindbergh became a national hero in the United States. At the age of 25, he had been the first person to make a solo flight across the Atlantic. "The Lone Eagle", as the press dubbed him, was modest, charming, and good-looking, and his fame lasted. Three years later, he and his wife Anne Morrow Lindbergh were America's golden couple, to such an extent that they felt compelled to flee from the public's admiring gaze. They built a house on a remote tract of land in New Jersey near the little town of Hopewell, and here, on June 22, 1930, their first child was born.

"The Eaglet", as the child came to be known, lived for less than two years. On the cold, rainy night of May 1, 1932, somewhere between 8 and 10 P.M., the little boy was kidnapped. Lindbergh was out hunting with his Springfield rifle for signs of the kidnapper when the State Police arrived, headed by their chief, H. Norman Schwarzkopf (father of "Stormin" Norman Schwarzkopf). Lindbergh had already found an envelope, but had not opened it. The police had no such qualms. Inside they found a ransom note in blue ink demanding $50,000. Details of where to place the money would follow. The police were not to be informed. Three days later another note arrived, raising the ransom to $70,000. Lindbergh was prepared to do whatever was asked for the return of his child. A further three days later, a certain John F. Condon offered his services as a go-between.

Condon was the first of many larger-than-life characters to become involved in the case. He was a windbag, a self-promoter, and a bungler, but Lindbergh and the kidnapper accepted his services. A meeting was arranged at the Woodlawn Cemetery in the Bronx with a man who called himself "Cemetery John", following which the child's sleeping suit was mailed to Lindbergh. A second meeting was arranged, attended by both Condon and Lindbergh. They heard Cemetery John

Lindbergh Baby

Charles Augustus Lindbergh Jnr. in happier days, before he became the most famous baby in the world.

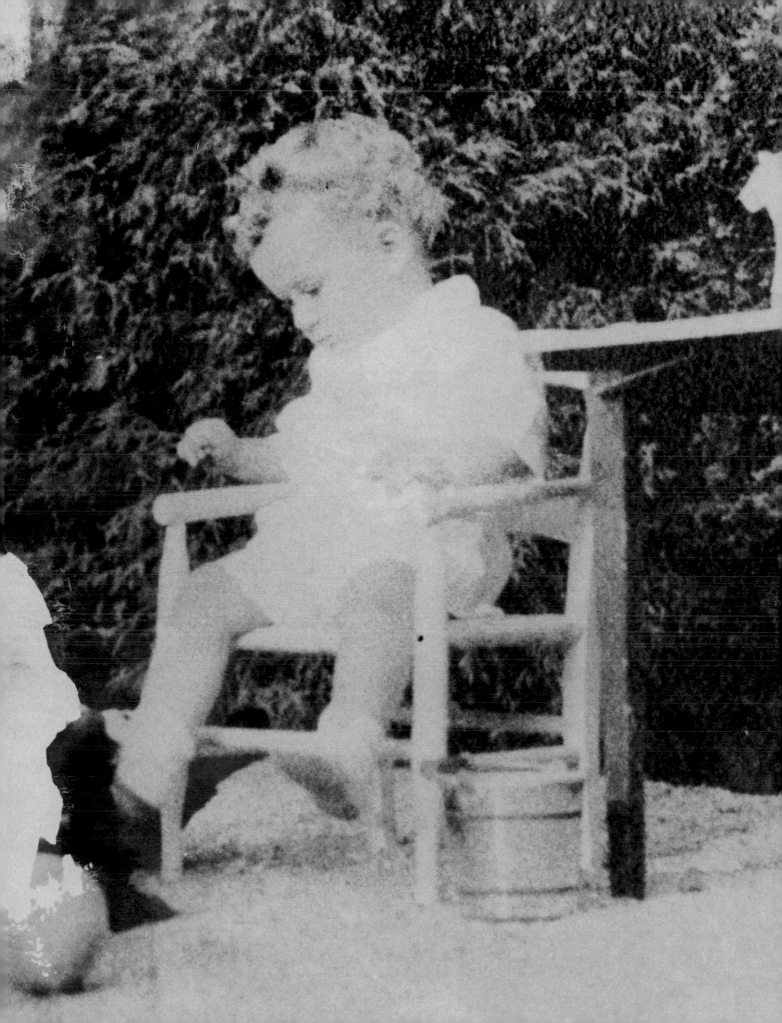

call to them in a strong German accent. Lindbergh handed over $50,000 in "gold notes", and received a note allegedly telling him where to find the victim. It was now over a month since the little boy had been taken.

The note was worthless. Another month was to pass before the body of Charles Jnr. was found, just six kilometres (four miles) from home. It was little more than a skeleton, hidden in a heap of rotting vegetation. The left leg, left hand, and right arm were missing. The cause of death was a massive fracture of the skull. It was a shocking discovery.

At first, one of the Lindbergh's servants was suspected of the crime. The poor woman was so upset by such an accusation that she killed herself, swallowing silver polish that

contained arsenic. Then Condon himself became a suspect. Schwarzkopf and his men tapped Condon's telephone, intercepted his mail, dug holes in his yard, and even stripped the paper from the walls of his house, before deciding he was eccentric, but not guilty.

And then, almost a year after the discovery of the body, some of the ransom money turned up at a gas station in the Bronx. The gas station manager thought it odd that a customer should pay for 98 cents of gas with a $10 bill, and noted the license plate number on the car. It turned out to be registered to a man named Bruno Hauptmann, a German who had entered the States illegally in 1923.

Hauptmann's trial, acerbically labelled "the greatest story since the Resurrection" by H. L. Mencken, was held in Fleming, New Jersey. Right to the end, the Crime of the Century threw up bizarre, oversize characters. The prosecuting Attorney General, David T. Wilenz, was a mixture of dandy and bully, after the style of Al Capone. The defence counsel, Edward J. Reilly, was a bully, a womanizer, and a boozer, whose afternoon performances in court were remarkably listless. Two weeks after the verdict, Reilly was taken to a Brooklyn hospital in a straitjacket.

Hauptmann was found guilty. In the little time between sentence and execution, he was vilified in the press, but later doubts were voiced as to the justice of his trial and sentence. For 60 years, up to her death in 1994, his widow Anna persisted that he had been innocent. As for the Lindberghs, they had another son, and left the United States to settle in Europe, where the "Lone Eagle" sadly became a great admirer of Hermann Göring and the Luftwaffe.

(top left) Charles Lindbergh on the morning of the opening of Hauptmann's trial. (left) Bruno Hauptmann leaves New York Police Headquarters, September 21, 1934. (top right) Newspaper reporters and members of the public surround the spot where the Lindbergh baby's body was found, four miles from the Lindbergh home. (right) The handwriting evidence that did much to convict Hauptmann. The lower "signature" was constructed from letters taken from the ransom note.

Hauptmann Signature	
Anonymous Letters	

On February 4, 1974, 19-year-old Patty Hearst was abducted from the apartment she shared with her partner in Berkeley, California. Her kidnappers were members of the Symbionese Liberation Army (SLA), an American para-military group with revolutionary ideals. Their aim was to hold her until other members of the SLA were released from prison. They had chosen Patty because she was the granddaughter of the newspaper tycoon, William Randolph Hearst. Negotiations for the exchange failed, however, and the SLA then demanded the distribution of $6 million worth of food among the poor of the Bay Area of California. The Hearst family complied with this request, but the SLA did not release Patty.

A few weeks later, however, Patty appeared in a new guise. On April 15 she was caught on a surveillance camera, wielding an assault rifle and participating in the robbery of the Sunset District branch of the Hibernia National Bank in San Francisco. Perhaps coincidentally, perhaps not, when Patty had attended the Santa Catalina School for Girls in Monterey, she had been friends with Patricia Tobin, whose family had founded the Hibernia National Bank. Following the robbery, Patty sent messages saying that she was now committed to the goals of the SLA.

In September 1975, she was arrested. Four months later, she was brought to trial. Her defence was that she had been physically and sexually abused by her captors, and also brainwashed so that she had no option but to join them. It was not a convincing defence and was poorly presented by her attorney, whom some allege was drunk during the trial. What happened may have been an extreme case of the "Stockholm syndrome", where captives identify with their captors. In any event, Patty Hearst was found guilty. Three years later, her sentence was commuted by President Jimmy Carter, and she was released in 1979. In January 2001, she was granted a full pardon by Bill Clinton on the last day of his Presidency.

Patty Hearst

The surveillance camera image of American heiress Patty Hearst taking part in a San Francisco bank robbery, April 15, 1974.

In 1977 a story broke that had tabloid reporters in Britain drooling. The story was: ex-Miss Wyoming fails to seduce pop star, joins Church of the Latter Day Saints, abducts young Mormon missionary, forces him to have kinky sex, is charged with kidnap, jumps bail and disappears. The ex-beauty queen was Joyce McKinney. The pop star, who showed good judgement in not falling for her charms, was Wayne Osmond. The poor abused Mormon was 21-year-old Kirk Anderson. Also involved was McKinney's partner in crime, Keith May. What gave the story even more zest was that while May was obsessed with McKinney, she cared not a jot for him, being obsessed with Anderson. It was a *ménage a trois* of spectacularly complicated proportions.

The press could not believe its luck. Here was a beautiful, intelligent and highly-articulate woman prepared to tell all in a seductive Southern drawl that made what she said all the more exciting. And here was a victim who corroborated her story in fine detail. Anderson told those in the suburban courtroom at Epsom, Surrey, that he had been taken by May and McKinney to a lonely cottage, and tied to a bed with leather straps, padlocks, chains, and ropes. "She grabbed my pyjamas and tore them from my body," he said. "She proceeded to have intercourse. I did not want it to happen. I was very upset."

McKinney endorsed Anderson's account. "Kirk has to be tied up to have an orgasm," she said. "The thought of being powerless before a woman seems to excite him." Later she made the strength of her own feelings perfectly clear. "I loved Kirk so much that I would have skied down Mount Everest in the nude with a carnation up my nose."

It never came to that. The trial was fixed for May 1978. By then McKinney had fled to the States, via Ireland and Canada, and in her absence, she was sentenced to a year's imprisonment. She never reappeared, leaving the press to dream and mourn "The Story That Got Away".

Joyce McKinney

In a police van taking her to court, a distraught Joyce McKinney holds up her version of what happened, November 23, 1977.

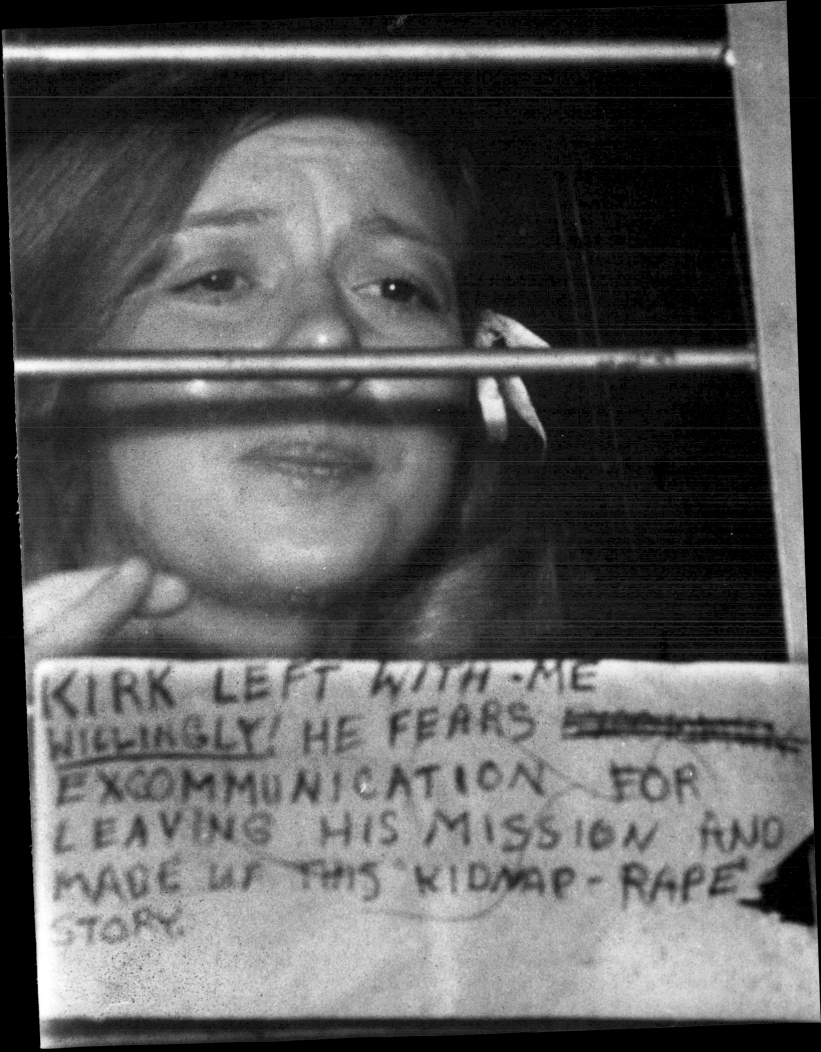

Index

Picture Acknowledgements

Even with 70 million images to choose from amongst the vast archives and collections of Getty Images the editors' task for this project was daunting. Much thanks go to our colleagues at Agence France Presse, to Jeff Burak and Michelle Franklin at Time & Life Pictures, and to Mitch Blank and Kristeen Ballard at Getty Images in New York.

The Editors also wish to thank Topham Picturepoint for supplying the pictures on pages 79, 191, 195 and 197. All other pictures are courtesy of the various collections either held or represented by Getty Images. Those requiring further attribution are indicated as follows

Key
t top **m** middle **b** bottom **l** left **r** right **i** inset

AFP Agence France Presse **AS** American Stock **CNP** Consolidated News Pictures **ICP** International Centre of Photography **LOC** Library of Congress **NA** National Archives **NYT** New York Times Co. **T&LP** Time & Life Pictures

2 Vernon Merritt III/T&LP; **8-9, 12tr, 12bl** AS; **13t** LOC #3a50864; **14t** John Swartz/AS; **18-19** AS; **21** Mansell/T&LP; **25br** AS; **28tr** NYT; **28b** Herb and Dorothy McLaughlin; **31** AS; **35t** AFP; **35b** T&LP; **36-7** NYT; **38-9** Francis Miller/T&LP; **41** Allan Grant/T&LP; **44b** Dennis Oulds; **47tl** Paul S Howell; **47tr** Dave Einsel; **47bl** Pam Francis; **47br** James Nielsen/AFP; **48-9** Ian Cook/T&LP; **51** Richard Howard/T&LP; **57** AS; **67** Ed Clark/T&LP; **69** Yale Joel/T&LP; **71** Ralph Crane/T&LP; **72t** State of Mississippi Attorney General's Office; **72b** Kyle Carter; **73** NA; **75** Beth Keiser; **81** LAPD; **82t** Jean-Marc Giboux; **82b** LAPD/AFP; **83t** AFP; **83b** Richard Creamer; **84** Vince Bucci/AFP; **85** AFP; **90-1** David Lees/T&LP; **89** Jacob A Riis/Museum of the City of New York; **95-7** George Silk/T&LP; **99** T&LP; **103** Hank Walker/T&LP; **107-9** Weegee (Arthur Fellig)/ICP; **111** Hank Walker/T&LP; **114t** Slim Aarons; **117** AS; **119** Carl Iwasaki/T&LP; **121, 123b, 124b** Fotos International; **122-3** Vernon Merritt III/T&LP; **124tl** Terry O'Neill; **124tr** Ralph Crane/T&LP; **125** Julian Wasser/T&LP; **127** David Hume Kennerly; **129** Yvonne Hemsey; **131** Mark Perlstein/T&LP; **137** Dimitar Dilkoff/AFP; **138** Jerry Lampen/AFP; **139** Savo Prelevic/AFP; **133** Tim Roberts/AFP; **134l** Bob Daemmrich/AFP; **134-5** Jim Bourg; **141** Steve Liss/T&LP; **143** Clark County Sheriff's Department/AFP; **145** FBI; **146** Bob Houlihan/US Navy; **147** Peter C Brandt; **148** Mario Tama; **149** Stan Honda/AFP; **151, 152bl, br** Jefferson County Sheriff's Department; **152tl** T&LP; **152-3** Mark Leffingwell/AFP; **154-5** Scott Peterson; **169** Ralph Morse/T&LP; **171** AFP; **173, 176tmr, 177tr** Francis Miller/T&LP; **174-7 (all except 176tmr, 177tr)** Frank Scherschel/T&LP; **179** Carl Iwasaki/T&LP; **182-3** Art Rickerby/T&LP; **185** Art Shay/T&LP; **187** Des Plaines Police Department, IL; **189** Paul Hawthorne; **199** Elaine Thompson; **201** Texas Department of Corrections/AFP; **203** Barbara Laing/T&LP; **205** Florida Department of Corrections; **207-9** Terry Smith/T&LP; **211** Bo Rader; **213** Eugene Garcia/AFP; **214-5** Taro Yamasaki/T&LP; **216-17** Makaram Gad Alkareem/AFP; **220l** LOC #3a53289; **220r** LOC 3g05341; **221t** LOC #02961; **221b (l-r)** LOC #04208, #3g06468, #04213, #04221, #04217, #04218; **222-3** LOC #04230; **225** Mansell/T&LP; **227** Austrian State Archives/Imagno; **230t, br** Mansell/T&LP; **233** Bilderwelt/Roger-Viollet; **238** Art Rickerby/T&LP; **239t** Carl Mydans/T&LP; **239b** CBS Photo Archive; **240t** NA; **240b** T&LP; **241** Shel Hershorn/T&LP; **244b** Santi Visalli Inc.; **245t** Joseph Louw/T&LP; **245b** Henry Groskinsky/T&LP; **247** Bill Eppridge/T&LP; **249** Luiz Alberto; **251** AFP; **252tl** Michael Evans/CNP; **252bl** Dirck Halstead; **254-5** Weegee (Arthur Fellig)/ICP; **259** Hank Walker/T&LP; **261** Henry Groskinsky/T&LP; **263** John Chiasson; **265** AFP; **267** Washington Police Department; **269** Al Golub; **270-1** Ed Lallo/T&LP; **275** AS; **279, 280t** Ed Clark/T&LP; **283** Terry O'Neill; **284tl** George Cordell; **284tr** Aubrey Hart; **287** Marianne Barcellona/T&LP; **289** T&LP; **290-1** Mickey Pfleger/T&LP; **299** CNP; **301** Frank Barratt